Man in the Kitchen

Recipes compiled by D. E. O'Neal

This recipe book contains recipes that have been collected from various sources. They have not been thoroughly or systematically tested by the author. D. E. O'Neal, publisher, printer-distributor or seller of this book is not responsible for errors or omissions.

Cover Design and Dividers by D. E. O'Neal.

Calligraphy by Ramona Spain-Gergle.

International Standard Book Number: 0-9626482-0-5

First Printing - September 1990
Second Printing - July 1992
Third Printing - December 1994

For additional copies write to:
Star-Daze Productions
1526 Mabry Mill
Houston, Texas 77062

Printed in the USA by

WIMMER
The Wimmer Companies, Inc.
Memphis • Dallas

Introduction

Man In The Kitchen Texas Style! is a unique collection of recipes compiled for the man who enjoys preparing and serving delicious Lone Star food.

Recipes were contributed by family and friends. Many of the recipes have been brought to Texas by different cultures who have settled in our great state. They have been passed down through the years; some remaining unchanged, while others have been adapted to satisfy the tastes of today's Texans!

Recipes vary from One Dish Savory Spaghetti for the busy man, to a more timely preparation of Shrimp Creole. Appetizers and beverages are included for the man who enjoys entertaining. The man with a sweet tooth will be pleased to find an abundance of recipes for cakes, cookies and desserts galore!

From the gourmet cook to the backyard chef, *Man In The Kitchen Texas Style!* will appeal to all men whether cooking for pleasure or just for survival!

COOK AND ENJOY!

D. E. O'Neal

☆

A Man with an Apron is a Man
Whose Kitchen is Filled with Temptation!

Table of Contents

Hot Broccoli Dip

3	stalks celery, chopped fine	1	10-ounce box frozen
2	green onions, chopped		chopped broccoli
1	4-ounce can mushrooms, drained	1	10¾-ounce can cream of mushroom soup
2	tablespoons margarine, melted	1	6-ounce roll garlic cheese spread

Sauté celery, onion and mushrooms in melted margarine. Cook broccoli according to package directions; drain well. Combine celery mixture, broccoli and soup. Melt cheese in double boiler or microwave; stir in broccoli mixture. Place in fondue pot to serve.

Cheese Ball

1	8-ounce package cream cheese, softened	2	tablespoons chopped green onion, with tops
1	8-ounce package sharp Cheddar cheese	1	tablespoon seasoned salt
2	cups chopped pecans	1	8½-ounce can crushed pineapple, (optional)
¼	cup finely chopped green pepper		

Cream cheeses together. Add remaining ingredients and mix well. Shape into cheese ball. Chill 6 to 8 hours. Serve with snack crackers.

Cheese Log

1	3-ounce package cream cheese	⅛	teaspoon red pepper
1	8-ounce package Cheddar cheese	¼	cup finely chopped pecans
1	tablespoon lemon juice	1	teaspoon chili powder
¼	teaspoon garlic powder	1	teaspoon paprika
		½	cup finely chopped pecans (to roll log in)

Let cheeses stand at room temperature until soft. Mix all ingredients together (save ½ cup pecans) and roll in a log roll. Sprinkle with ½ cup chopped pecans. Wrap in foil and chill in refrigerator.

Guacamole

3	ripe avocados	1	tablespoon lemon juice
1	fresh tomato, chopped		salt and pepper to taste
4	tablespoons sour cream		

Remove skin from avocado. Cut in half and discard seed. Place in a bowl and mash with a fork. Add chopped tomato, sour cream and lemon juice. Salt and pepper to taste. Serve with crisp tortillas.

Mexican Layered Party Dip

2	10½-ounce cans bean dip	2	tomatoes, chopped
2	avocados, chopped	1	cup green onions, with
3	tablespoons lemon juice		tops, chopped
1	8-ounce carton sour cream	2	cups Cheddar cheese,
½	cup mayonnaise		grated
1	package taco seasoning	½	cup chopped olives
	mix		

Spread bean dip on bottom of a 9x12-inch serving dish. Mix avocados with lemon juice and spread over bean dip. Mix sour cream, mayonnaise and taco seasoning. Spread over avocados. Place tomatoes and green onions over the sour cream mixture. Top with cheese and olives. Refrigerate 1 hour. Serve with tortilla chips.

Sausage Cheese Dip

1	pound bulk sausage	1	tablespoon Worcestershire
1	small onion, chopped	2	jalapeño peppers, chopped
2	pounds pasteurized		fine
	process cheese spread	2	tablespoons chili powder
1	10-ounce can tomatoes		
	and green chilies		

Lightly brown sausage and drain well. Add onion and cook until tender. Add remaining ingredients and cook over low heat until cheese melts. Stir often. Serve in fondue dish to keep hot.

Shrimp Dip

1   8-ounce package cream
    cheese, softened
1   cup finely chopped cooked
    shrimp
2   teaspoons lemon juice
2   teaspoons Worcestershire
    sauce

½   teaspoon horseradish
¼   teaspoon paprika
1   teaspoon lemon pepper
½   teaspoon garlic salt
2   tablespoons milk

Mix milk with softened cream cheese. Add remaining ingredients. Chill.

Spinach Con Queso

1   10-ounce package frozen
    chopped spinach, thawed
    and drained well
1   pound pasteurized process
    cheese spread

¼   cup milk
2   jalapeño peppers, chopped
    fine
1   10-ounce can tomatoes
    and chilies

Slowly melt cheese and milk together. Add remaining ingredients. Stir well.
Heat and serve warm with tortilla chips.

Vegetable Dip

1   16-ounce carton sour
    cream
1   8-ounce jar mayonnaise
1   teaspoon garlic powder

1   teaspoon red pepper
2   tablespoons chives
1   tablespoon lemon juice
1   tablespoon season all

Mix ingredients together and chill in refrigerator. Serve with your choice of
vegetables: carrots, green pepper, broccoli, cauliflower, squash, cucum-
bers, celery, radishes, etc.

Chee-Zees

2	sticks oleo	2	cups crispy rice cereal
2	cups flour	1	10-ounce package mild
½	teaspoon red cayenne pepper		Cheddar cheese, grated

Cream oleo, flour and red pepper together. Add crispy rice cereal and Cheddar cheese. Form into 1-inch balls. Place on ungreased cookie sheet and bake in 350 degree oven 20 minutes. Remove and cool.

☆

Mexican Pinwheels

20	flour tortillas	1	tablespoon lime juice
2	8-ounce packages cream cheese, softened	3	mild jalapeño peppers, chopped
½	pint sour cream		
4	green onions, finely chopped		

Let cream cheese sit at room temperature to soften. Mix cream cheese, sour cream, onions, peppers and lime juice. Spread on tortillas. Roll each tortilla like a jelly roll. Cut into ⅓-inch thick slices. Stack on serving dish. Cover with a damp cloth and refrigerate 1 hour or overnight. Serve with hot sauce for dipping.

☆

Ham Kabobs

1	1½ pound ham steak, cooked, cut into 1-inch cubes	16	large pimento-stuffed olives
1	small pineapple, peeled, cored and cut into 1-inch cubes	1	cup brown sugar
		½	cup honey
		½	cup orange juice
		¼	cup pineapple juice

Combine brown sugar, honey, orange juice and pineapple juice; mix well and set aside. Alternate ham, pineapple and olives on skewers. Grill over medium heat 10 to 12 minutes; turning often. Baste liberally with honey mixture after each turn. Yield: 4 servings.

Party Franks

1	cup catsup	36	cocktail sausages
1	cup currant or red plum jelly	1	13½-ounce can pineapple chunks, drained
1	tablespoon lemon juice		
4	tablespoons prepared mustard		

Combine all ingredients except sausages and pineapple. Blend well. Add sausages and pineapple chunks. Simmer over low heat 15 to 20 minutes. Serve with cocktail toothpicks.

Pigs In A Blanket

1   10-count can flaky biscuits   20   cocktail sausages

Pull each biscuit apart horizontally. Place 1 sausage on top of each biscuit and roll like a jelly roll. Place sealed side down on greased cookie sheet. Bake at 400 degrees for 10 to 15 minutes or until golden brown.

☆

Pizza Snacks

2	English muffins	catsup
4	slices cheese	oregano
	Parmesan cheese	

Toast muffin on cookie sheet. Spread 1 tablespoon catsup over each muffin half. Cover with 1 slice of cheese and a few pinches of oregano. Cook in 350 degree oven until the cheese has melted. Optional toppings: Sliced ham, browned ground meat, bell peppers, onions and mushrooms.

Sautéed Mushrooms

3	pounds fresh mushrooms	⅛	teaspoon salt
1	medium size onion,	6	ounces red cooking wine
	chopped	1	stick oleo
3	tablespoons garlic juice		

Clean mushrooms. Mix remaining ingredients and mushrooms together. Cook over low heat for 3 hours. Serve.

Collin's Stuffed Mushrooms

2	pounds fresh mushrooms	1	small box frozen spinach
2	tablespoons butter	½	pound Monterey Jack
⅓	cup onion, chopped fine		cheese, grated
½	cup mushroom stems, diced	½	pound sausage

Cut off mushroom stems. Sauté onions and stems in butter. Cook sausage and drain. Cook spinach according to package directions and drain. Mix all ingredients together. Stuff mushrooms. Place in a shallow greased baking dish. Bake at 350 degrees for 15 minutes.

☆

Beer Batter Fried Onion Rings

1½	cups flour	½	teaspoon red cayenne
1½	cups beer, active or flat, cold or warm		pepper
			oil for frying
3	large onions		

Mix flour and beer in a bowl and stir until well blended. Let sit at room temperature for 3 to 4 hours. Peel onions and slice. Sprinkle with pepper. Dip onion rings into batter and place in hot oil. Turn once or twice until golden brown. Drain on paper towels.

Nachos

36	to 45 tortilla chips	36	to 45 pieces of sliced
2	cups shredded Monterey		jalapeño peppers
	Jack cheese	¼	teaspoon chili powder

Arrange chips on a 9x15-inch glass dish. Sprinkle cheese over chips. Top with peppers and sprinkle with chili powder. Broil in hot oven or microwave until cheese melts.

Sausage Pinwheels

1	pound bulk pork sausage,	2	cups biscuit mix
	hot or mild	½	cup water

Mix biscuit mix with water. On a floured surface, roll dough into a rectangle. Spread with sausage and roll in a jelly roll. Chill in refrigerator. Remove and slice roll in ¼ inch slices. Place on cookie sheet and bake in 400 degree oven for 10 to 15 minutes. Remove from pan.

☆

Sausage Squares

1	pound sausage, crumble, brown and drain	1	pint half and half milk
1	8-ounce package shredded Cheddar cheese	12	slices bread butter to spread over top of bread
8	eggs		

Butter baking sheet and place 6 slices of bread in pan. Sprinkle browned, drained sausage over bread. Spread shredded cheese over sausage. Top with remaining bread slices. Butter top of bread. Beat eggs and half and half milk together. Pour over the top of bread and around the edge of pan. Cover and refrigerate overnight. Bake for 1 hour in 350 degree oven. Remove and serve hot.

Sausage Balls

1	pound sharp Cheddar cheese, grated	1	teaspoon red pepper
1	pound hot bulk sausage	3½	cups biscuit mix

Mix all ingredients together. Roll into 100 very small balls. Place on ungreased cookie sheet and bake in 350 degree oven for 20 minutes. Remove and cool.

Vegetable Pizza

2	packages refrigerated crescent rolls	1	cup chopped celery
½	teaspoon onion salt	1	cup shredded carrots
2	8-ounce packages cream cheese	1	cup green peppers
1	cup sour cream	1	cup broccoli
1	tablespoon onion flakes	1	cup cauliflower
1	tablespoon dill weed	1	cup radishes, sliced
1	tablespoon chopped parsley	1	tablespoon chopped chives
		1	cup shredded cheese

Spread rolls on pizza pan or cookie sheet. Bake at 375 degrees for 10 minutes. Cool. Beat onion salt, cream cheese, onion flakes, sour cream, dill weed and chopped parsley together. Smooth on cooled crust. Place vegetables over creamed cheese mixture. Top with shredded cheese. Store in refrigerator.

Caramel Corn

2	cups brown sugar	1	teaspoon imitation butter flavoring
2	sticks oleo		
½	cup white corn syrup	12	to 14 cups popped corn
1	teaspoon salt		(1½ cups unpopped)
½	teaspoon soda		

Bring sugar, oleo, syrup and salt to boil. Boil 5 minutes. Stir in flavoring and soda. Pour over popped corn and stir to coat well. Pour into a large roasting pan and bake one hour at 250 degrees, stirring every 15 minutes during baking. Remove from oven and cool, stirring every 5 minutes. When cool, store in an airtight container.

Bar-B-Qued Pecans

2   tablespoons apple cider vinegar
3   tablespoons honey

1   teaspoon brown sugar
4   tablespoons melted butter
    pecan halves

Pour cider vinegar, honey and brown sugar into a pint jar with lid. Mix thoroughly. Fill jar with pecan halves. Shake until all pecans are coated. Pour pecans on cookie sheet and spread out evenly. Place under broiler for 5 to 10 minutes being careful not to burn. Remove from oven and brush with melted butter. Bake in 300 degree oven for 15 minutes. Cool and store in airtight container.

Sugary Peanuts

1   cup water
1   cup sugar

3   cups raw, unblanched peanuts

Combine water and sugar in large saucepan. Cook over medium heat until sugar dissolves - will be clear. Add peanuts and continue cooking, stirring frequently until all syrup has been absorbed by peanuts, approximately 20 to 30 minutes. Spread on buttered baking sheet. Bake in 300 degree oven for one hour, stirring every 10 to 15 minutes. Remove and cool. Store in airtight container.

Texas Trash

Mix:

1   box crispy rice cereal squares
1   box crispy corn cereal squares

1   large bag pretzels
1   large bag pork skins
3   cups pecan halves

Sauce:

1   cup margarine, melted
1   cup bacon drippings
1   tablespoon celery salt
1   tablespoon garlic powder

1   tablespoon seasoned salt
1   tablespoon Worcestershire
    dash hot pepper sauce

Pour dry ingredients into large baking dish. Mix sauce and pour over dry ingredients, coating well. Bake 2 to 3 hours in 225 degree oven, stirring every 15 minutes. Remove from oven. Cool and store in airtight container.

Fruit Dip

1   7-ounce jar marshmallow creme
1   8-ounce package cream cheese

1   8-ounce carton sour cream
1   14-ounce can sweetened condensed milk

Mix all ingredients together and place in a blender. Blend until smooth. Remove and refrigerate 1 hour. Serve with assorted fruits. Yield: 4 cups.

☆

Frosted Grapes

1   egg white, slightly beaten
small bunches of seedless grapes, red or green

sugar

Brush beaten egg white over each cluster of grapes. Make sure each grape is covered. Sprinkle with sugar and place on cookie sheet. Let dry for 2 hours or until sugar coating becomes hard and crunchy.

☆

Fruit Kabobs

36   mandarin orange slices
24   fresh strawberries
24   green seedless grapes
24   fresh pineapple chunks
½   cup sour cream

½   cup marshmallow creme
2   teaspoons grated orange rind
1   teaspoon ginger

Thread fruit onto 12 (8-inch) bamboo skewers; chill. Combine remaining ingredients, mixing well; serve as a dip with fruit kabobs. Yield: 12 kabobs.

Whitney's Fruit Pizza

Crust:
1   roll sugar cookie dough

Filling:
1   8-ounce package soft   ½ cup sugar
     cream cheese   1   teaspoon vanilla

Fruit:
     strawberries   mandarin oranges, drained
     bananas   (reserve juice)
     chunk pineapple, drained   green grapes
     (reserve juice)   lemon juice

Glaze:
     juice from drained pine-   2   teaspoons minute tapioca
     apple and oranges

Slice cookie dough and place on pizza pan. Press evenly over pan. Bake like a large cookie. Mix cream cheese, sugar and vanilla. Spread over cooled crust. Squeeze lemon juice over bananas to retain color. Starting with the outer edge, place a row of strawberries on pizza, second row bananas, third row pineapple, fourth row oranges, fifth row green grapes and ending with strawberries in the center. Glaze: Pour juice from pineapple and mandarin oranges in pan. Add 2 teaspoons minute tapioca and heat to thicken. Cool and spread over fruit pizza. Store in refrigerator.

Chocolate Covered Strawberries

white or dark chocolate   large strawberries with
                                   stems

Melt chocolate very slowly over low heat. Wash berries and drain. Dip berry into chocolate, covering evenly. Note: Use toothpick if berry does not have stem. After dipping in chocolate, place on wax paper. Place in refrigerator to set.

Champagne Punch

1	25.4-ounce bottle champagne, chilled	2	33.8-ounce bottles ginger ale
2	cups orange juice	15	maraschino cherries
2	cups pineapple juice		orange slices
1	6-ounce can frozen pink lemonade, thawed		

Pour 1 bottle of ginger ale and thawed lemonade into an 11 cup ring. Add cherries and freeze until firm. Unmold ice ring into a punch bowl. Add remaining ingredients. Stir well. Serves 15 to 20.

Cranberry Punch

1	pound cranberries	2	sticks cinnamon
1	quart water	6	cloves

Mix together and simmer on low heat for 45 minutes. Strain through colander or sieve. Mix cranberry juice with:

⅔	cup lemon juice	2½	cups water
2½	cups sugar		

Mix well. Serve hot or cold. Yields: 1 gallon.

Lime Punch

5	6-ounce packages lime gelatin	2	quarts pineapple juice
1	20-ounce can crushed pineapple	5	cups sugar
1	12-ounce can grapefruit juice	5	cups water
		8	quarts ginger ale
			juice of 24 lemons

Mix all ingredients together except ginger ale. Freeze. When ready to serve, add ginger ale.

Island Punch

½	ounce white rum	1	ounce pineapple juice
¼	ounce gold rum	1	teaspoon lime juice
1	ounce apricot liqueur		orange slices and cherries
2	ounces orange juice		to garnish

Mix first six ingredients together. Pour over ice in chilled glass. Garnish with orange slices and cherries.

Strawberry Punch

1	6-ounce can frozen lemonade, thawed	1	8-ounce can crushed pineapple
2	cups frozen strawberries		ginger ale

Place first 3 ingredients in a 5 cup blender. Fill with ginger ale and ice cubes. Blend. Serve immediately!

Party Punch

An All Time Favorite

2	6-ounce packages cherry gelatin	13	cups boiling water

Mix together and add:

6	cups sugar	6	cups hot water

Let cool slightly and add juices and extract.

1	24-ounce bottle lemon juice	1	ounce almond extract
3	46-ounce cans pineapple juice	3	bottles ginger ale

Mix together and freeze in plastic containers for 24 to 36 hours. When ready to use, let thaw for about 2 hours or until it can be broken up with a fork. Add 3 bottles ginger ale. Mix well until slushy. Serve.

Sunny Day Punch

4	cups water	2	4 to 5 quart bottles champagne, chilled
3	cups unsweetened pineapple juice		orange slices and mint leaves to garnish
1	6-ounce can frozen orange juice concentrate, thawed		
1	6-ounce can frozen lemon-ade concentrate, thawed		

Combine water, pineapple juice, orange juice and lemonade concentrate. Stir well. Chill thoroughly. Pour into punch bowl and slowly pour champagne down side of bowl. Stir gently to mix. Garnish with orange slices and mint leaves.

Percolator Punch

Great for cold days!

9	cups pineapple juice	9	cups cranberry juice
1	cup brown sugar	3	sticks cinnamon
1	teaspoon whole cloves		

Place juices and brown sugar in a 30-cup coffee maker. Place cinnamon and cloves in the basket. Plug in the coffee maker and perk.

Teetotaler's Punch

2	bananas	2	tablespoons lemon juice
2	cups crushed pineapple, undrained	10	maraschino cherries lemon-lime carbonated beverage
2	cups orange juice		
1	cup sugar		

Mix first five ingredients together in blender and blend. Stir in cherries. Freeze in 3 divided ice cube trays. When frozen, store cubes in plastic bags in freezer. To serve, place 3 or 4 cubes in a tall glass and fill with lemon-lime carbonated beverage.

Banana Split Float

1	pint fresh strawberries		scoops of chocolate and
2	ripe medium size bananas		strawberry ice cream
1	pint vanilla ice cream		whipped cream
3	cups cold milk		chopped pecans

Place strawberries and bananas in blender and mash. Add vanilla ice cream. Beat until blended. Add milk. Pour into chilled glasses and top with scoops of chocolate and strawberry ice cream. Add a scoop of whipped cream and top with pecans.

☆

Banana Smoothies

2	cups ice cubes	½	pineapple, frozen and cut
3	cups raspberry-apple cider		into cubes
2	bananas, frozen		

Pour all ingredients into 1½ quart blender. Blend until thick and creamy. Serves 4.

☆

Strawberry Smoothie

2	cups vanilla ice cream	2	teaspoons lemon juice
1½	cups fresh strawberries	2	cups crushed ice
2	tablespoons sugar	4	strawberries to garnish

Combine first 5 ingredients in container of an electric blender; process until smooth. Pour into individual glasses and garnish with strawberries. Serve immediately. Yield: 4 cups.

☆

Hot Chocolate Mix

16	cups instant milk (1 large box)	6	ounces instant dairy creamer
16	ounces instant chocolate drink mix	4	cups powdered sugar

Mix and store in airtight container. Mix ½ cup per 1 cup boiling water. For Mexican Hot Chocolate: Add 4 heaping tablespoons cinnamon to mix.

Chocolate Malt

1	cup cold milk	1	quart vanilla ice cream,
2	tablespoons powdered chocolate malt		softened
1	tablespoon chocolate flavoring for milk		

Place electric blender container in freezer to chill. Combine all ingredients in container and process until smooth. Pour into chilled glasses to serve. Yield: 4 cups.

Spiced Tea

1	quart weak tea	1	cup lemon juice
2	3-ounce packages straw-berry or lemon gelatin	1	quart water
½	gallon boiling water	2	cups sugar
6	cinnamon sticks	1	46-ounce can pineapple juice
12	cloves		juice of 4 oranges
1	pint water	1	teaspoon allspice

Dissolve gelatin in boiling water. Set aside. Simmer cinnamon sticks, cloves and 1 pint water for 20 minutes. Mix all ingredients together. Heat but do not boil. Yield: 30 servings.

Brandied Coffee Punch

4	cups milk	½	teaspoon cloves
½	cup sugar	2	teaspoons vanilla
1	teaspoon cinnamon	1	quart coffee ice cream
4	cups brewed coffee	1	cup brandy

In a large saucepan, heat milk to scalding. Remove from heat and combine with coffee, sugar, spices and vanilla. Refrigerate to chill. When ready to serve, spoon ice cream into punch bowl. Add brandy and stir in chilled coffee mixture. Serve immediately. Yields: 12 1-cup servings.

Hot Spiced Holiday Punch

1	cup water	1	18-ounce can grapefruit
⅔	cup sugar		juice
2	sticks cinnamon	2	cups orange juice
1	teaspoon whole cloves	½	cup lemon juice
1	teaspoon whole allspice	2	cups rosé wine
1	46-ounce can pineapple		orange slices to garnish
	juice		

Combine water, sugar, cinnamon, cloves and allspice in a saucepan. Boil 3 minutes. Strain out spices. Add juices and wine. Heat until hot. Do not boil. Serve hot and garnish with orange slices.

Hot Spiced Apple Cider

1	gallon apple cider	1	teaspoon ground cloves
1	12-ounce can frozen	1	teaspoon nutmeg
	lemonade	1	cup sugar
2	teaspoons cinnamon		

Mix all ingredients together. Heat, but do not boil. Serve hot.

☆

Wassail

2	quarts sweet apple cider	1	stick whole cinnamon
2	cups orange juice	1	teaspoon whole cloves
1	cup lemon juice	1	cup sugar, honey or brown
5	cups pineapple juice		sugar to taste

Combine all ingredients and bring to a simmer. Strain and serve hot. Makes about 16 8-ounce servings.

Old Fashioned Lemonade

1	7½-ounce bottle lemon juice from concentrate	6	cups ice water
1½	cups sugar	1	lemon, sliced

Mix all ingredients together in a half-gallon container. Stir until sugar is dissolved. Add ice to fill. Makes 2 quarts.

Hot Mexican Cider

2	quarts apple cider	⅓	cup orange-flavored
¼	cup lemon juice		liqueur
2	cups tequila		lemon slices to garnish

Combine cider and lemon juice in a large saucepan and cook over medium heat until mixture simmers. Add tequila and orange liqueur; cook until heated. Pour into individual mugs and garnish with lemon slices.

Eggnog

8	eggs	1	pint heavy cream
⅔	cup sugar		ground nutmeg
1	cup whiskey		

Separate eggs. Beat whites until frothy. Set aside. Beat yolks. Slowly add sugar and whiskey, beating well. Whip the cream. Fold in beaten egg whites and whipped cream. Serve in chilled glasses. Sprinkle nutmeg on top.

Irish Coffee

½	ounce Irish whiskey		strong dripped coffee
½	ounce rum		whipped cream
¼	teaspoon sugar		

In serving cup, stir whiskey, rum and sugar until sugar is dissolved. Fill with coffee. Top with whipped cream.

Bloody Mary

1	46-ounce can tomato juice, chilled	1	tablespoon Worcestershire sauce
2	cups vodka		pepper to taste
1	teaspoon salt		lime slices
	juice of 1 lemon		
1½	teaspoons hot pepper sauce		

Mix all ingredients except lime slices together. Chill in refrigerator. Fill glasses with ice. Squeeze a slice of lime in glass and drop the slice into the glass. Pour mixture over lime and ice. Makes approximately 6 glasses.

☆

Bob's Frozen Daiquiris

1	6-ounce can frozen lemonade	1	6-ounce can filled with rum

Place rum and lemonade in 40-ounce blender. Fill with ice and blend. Serve.

☆

Frozen Margaritas

1	6-ounce can frozen lime juice	6	ounces tequila
4	ounces triple sec		crushed ice to fill blender
			margarita salt for glass rim

Combine liquid ingredients in blender. Add crushed ice and blend. Serve in salt-rimmed glasses.

Piña Coladas

½   cup cream of coconut
1   cup unsweetened pine-
     apple juice, chilled

½   cup light rum
2   cups crushed ice
     whole cherries to garnish

Combine first four ingredients in a blender. Blend for ½ minute. Pour into 6 chilled cocktail glasses. Garnish with cherries.

Red Roosters

2½   cups vodka
1   32-ounce jar cranberry
     juice cocktail
1   12-ounce can frozen
     orange juice concentrate,
     thawed

4   cups water

Mix all ingredients together and freeze in a plastic container. To serve: Remove and spoon about 4 cups mixture into container of electric blender. Mix until mixture reaches desired consistency. Repeat with the remaining mixture. Yields: Approx. 3 quarts.

Southern Comfort

1   6-ounce can frozen orange
     juice concentrate, thawed
3½   cups chablis

1   cup water
½   cup triple sec
     orange slices

Mix first four ingredients together. Stir well and serve over ice. Garnish with orange slices. Yield: 6 cups.

Soups

Broccoli Cheese Soup

1	stick oleo, melted	2	cups evaporated milk
2	green onions, chopped fine	½	cup whole milk
1	cup celery, chopped fine	2	pounds pasteurized
½	cup carrots, chopped fine		process cheese spread,
½	cup broccoli, chopped fine		cut into small pieces
½	cup flour	½	teaspoon cayenne pepper
2	cups boiling water	1	teaspoon black pepper
2	cups chicken broth		

Sauté onions, celery, carrots and broccoli in oleo until soft. Stir in flour to coat vegetables well. Mix milk and chicken broth together in a separate pan. Heat until scalding around edge of pan. Gradually add boiling water and broth mixture to the vegetables. Add cheese and heat very slowly over low heat until the cheese is melted. Stir in cayenne and black pepper. Serve with hot cornbread.

Cheese Soup

1	stick butter	4	cups boiling water
½	cup minced green onions	4	cups chicken broth
2	cups minced celery	4	cups evaporated milk
2	cups minced carrots	2	cups homogenized milk
1	cup flour		salt and pepper to taste
4	pounds pasteurized		
	process cheese spread		

Sauté vegetables in butter until tender. Scald milk and broth together. Add flour to vegetables, mixing well. Add boiling water, scalded milk and broth. Stir well. Cut cheese into pieces and add to hot liquid mixture. Cook on low heat until cheese melts. Do not let boil or soup will curdle. Makes 1 gallon.

Chicken Noodle Soup

1	3 to 4 pound chicken, cut up	1	tablespoon salt
2	green onions, with tops, cut up	3	tablespoons butter
1	stalk celery, cut into 2-inch pieces	1	teaspoon pepper
		3½	quarts water

Place in large saucepan and cook for 45 minutes or until chicken is tender. Strain and discard vegetables. Remove chicken, debone and cut into bite size pieces.

Noodles:

1	egg	1	cup flour
2	tablespoons water		dash pepper
¼	teaspoon salt		

Beat egg, water, salt and pepper. Gradually add flour and knead slightly. Roll out on floured surface and cut into very thin strips. Add to broth and boil 15 minutes. Add chicken pieces. Yields: 8 servings.

☆

Five Hour Oven Stew

2	pounds boneless stew meat, cubed	1	onion, sliced
1	17 ounce can sweet peas	8	potatoes, cut into large pieces
5	carrots, sliced	1	bay leaf
1	can cream of tomato soup, thinned with ½ can water	2	tablespoons cooking oil
			flour, salt and pepper

Salt and pepper stew meat. Sprinkle with flour. Heat oil in frying pan. Brown meat. Remove and place in a large covered roasting pan. Add remaining ingredients and stir. Cover and bake at 250 degrees for 5 hours. Remove from oven. Remove bay leaf. Serve.

German Potato Soup

5	large new potatoes (red) peeled and diced	1	stick oleo
2	stalks celery, diced	2	tablespoons flour
2	green onions, with tops, chopped fine	½	cup milk
			salt and pepper to taste

Place potatoes, celery and onions in a large saucepan. Cover with water, approximately 3 cups. Boil until potatoes are tender. Melt oleo in a small frying pan over very low heat. Slowly mix in flour with a fork until smooth. Add to potatoes. Add milk and stir. Salt and pepper to taste. For a thinner soup, add more milk. Serves 4 to 6.

Hunter's Stew

1	pound ground chuck	2	medium potatoes, peeled and cubed
2	green onions, chopped		
1	10¾-ounce can condensed tomato soup		salt and pepper to taste
3	10¾-ounce cans vegetable soup		

Lightly brown ground chuck. In a large saucepan, place ground chuck and remaining ingredients. Cook 20 to 30 minutes or until potatoes are tender. Serve with crackers.

Lentil Bean Soup

1	16-ounce package lentils	3	teaspoons salt
6	slices bacon	1	teaspoon pepper
1	medium onion, chopped	1	green bell pepper, chopped
3	carrots, diced	½	teaspoon dried thyme
2	quarts water	2	bay leaves
3	stalks celery, chopped fine		

Wash lentils and place in a large saucepan. Add remaining ingredients and bring to a boil. Reduce heat and cook covered on low to medium heat approximately 3 hours. Add boiling water if needed as water boils down. Remove bay leaves.

Tortilla Soup

4	chicken breasts	1	teaspoon cumin
1	stick oleo	1	teaspoon salt
6	green onions, with tops, chopped	2	cloves garlic, minced
		1	teaspoon pepper
4	stalks celery, chopped	1	14-ounce can tomatoes
3	carrots, diced	1	17-ounce can whole kernel corn
2	fresh jalapeño peppers, seeded and chopped	½	cup flour
1	teaspoon chili powder	8	corn tortillas

Garnishes:

1	cup sour cream	1	cup grated Cheddar cheese
3	diced avocados		

Place chicken breasts in large saucepan or dutch oven. Cover with 4 to 5 cups water. Boil 30 minutes or until chicken is tender. Remove chicken and debone. Reserve broth. Melt oleo in a saucepan. Sauté onions, celery, carrots, peppers, garlic and chicken for about 5 minutes. Add chili powder, cumin, flour, salt and pepper. Pour into boiling chicken broth. Add tomatoes and corn. Reduce heat and simmer 45 minutes. Drop corn tortillas into melted shortening heated to 375 degrees. Fry until crisp. Drain on paper towels. Place a few tortilla strips in the bottom of 6 to 8 soup cups and add a spoon each of sour cream and avocado. Pour soup over mixture. Top with grated cheese. Serves 6 to 8.

☆

O'Neal's Chicken Rice Soup

4	chicken breasts	2	cups chopped celery
9	cups water	2	cups diced carrots
1	teaspoon salt	2	to 3 cups cooked rice
1	teaspoon pepper	4	chicken bouillon cubes
1	medium chopped onion, (optional)	2	pounds processed cheese

Place chicken breasts and water in large saucepan. Add salt, pepper, celery, onion and carrots. Cook 45 minutes until chicken is tender. Remove chicken and debone. Return chicken to broth and add rice and bouillon cubes. Cook for 1 hour over low heat. Add cheese and stir until melted. Serves 6 to 8.

Mama's Vegetable Soup

1½	pounds boneless stew meat	2	stalks celery, chopped
1	17-ounce can sweet peas	1	green bell pepper, chopped
1	16-ounce can cut green beans	1	medium onion, chopped
1	17-ounce can corn	1	1-pound package carrots, chopped
2	14½-ounce cans tomatoes	1	teaspoon basil
4	medium potatoes, peeled and cubed	½	teaspoon thyme
		2	teaspoons salt
		1	teaspoon pepper

Boil meat and carrots in a large pot approximately 1½ hours or until meat is tender. Add remaining ingredients and cook 30 more minutes or until potatoes are tender.

Texas Stew

10	wild turkeys, cleaned and cut in small pieces	1	bushel tomatoes, chopped
20	squirrels, cleaned and cut in small pieces	20	onions, chopped
2	rabbits (optional)	1	bushel new potatoes, peeled and chopped
1	bushel carrots, sliced	2	26-ounce boxes salt
		1	4-ounce can black pepper

Place turkey and squirrel pieces in a Texas size dutch oven. Add carrots, tomatoes, onions, potatoes, salt and pepper. Cover with water. Cook for two days over low heat. This will feed a Texas size crowd. To increase recipe, add 2 rabbits. Do this only if necessary, as most Texans do not like to find hare in their stew!

Borski's 24 Hour Bean Salad

1	15½-ounce can cut wax beans	1	bell pepper, sliced
1	16-ounce can kidney beans	½	cup salad oil
1	16-ounce can cut green beans	½	cup vinegar
1	red onion, sliced	½	cup sugar
		1	teaspoon salt
		1	teaspoon pepper

Drain liquids from beans and mix with salad oil, vinegar, sugar, salt and pepper. Mix beans, onion and bell pepper together. Pour liquid over bean mixture and stir well. Chill in refrigerator overnight.

Black-Eyed Pea Salad

2	16-ounce cans black-eyed peas, rinsed and drained	1	4-ounce jar pimiento, drained
1	cup chopped celery	1	8-ounce bottle Italian salad dressing
1	red bell pepper, chopped		
1	large tomato, peeled and chopped	4	slices bacon, cooked
3	green onions, chopped	2	green onions, diced fine

Combine first 7 ingredients. Place in covered container and chill overnight. Crumble bacon. Garnish salad with bacon and diced onions. Serves 8.

☆

Marinated Carrot Salad

2	pounds sliced frozen carrots, cooked and drained	1	teaspoon dry mustard
		1	10¾-ounce can tomato soup
1	onion, thinly sliced	1	teaspoon salt
1	green bell pepper, thinly sliced	1	teaspoon pepper
½	cup oil	1	teaspoon celery seed
¾	cup sugar	1	teaspoon Worcestershire sauce
¾	cup vinegar		

Mix first three ingredients in a large bowl. Mix remaining ingredients together and pour over carrot mixture. Refrigerate overnight.

Corn Salad

1	16-ounce can whole kernel corn, drained	½	cup celery, chopped
¼	cup green onions, with tops, chopped	½	cup shredded Cheddar cheese
½	cup bell pepper, chopped	½	cup thousand island dressing

Mix all ingredients together and chill in refrigerator overnight.

Cornbread Salad

2	packages cornbread mix	2	boiled eggs, chopped
5	green onions, with tops, chopped	2	jalapeño peppers, chopped, (optional)
1	medium bell pepper, chopped	1	cup mayonnaise
2	medium fresh tomatoes, chopped		salt and pepper to taste

Bake cornbread according to package directions. Cool. Crumble in a mixing bowl. Add remaining ingredients and toss lightly. Serves 6 to 8.

German Cole Slaw

1	medium head cabbage, shredded	1	cup sugar
1	medium onion, minced	1	green bell pepper, chopped fine
1	tablespoon celery seed		

Dressing:

¾	cup salad oil	2	tablespoons sugar
1	cup vinegar	1	teaspoon salt

Mix cabbage, onion, celery seed, sugar and bell pepper together. Bring dressing to a boil. Pour over cabbage and refrigerate overnight. Keeps for days in refrigerator.

English Pea Salad

1	15-ounce can peas, drained	3	tablespoons onion, chopped
2	hard-cooked eggs, chopped	5	slices cheese, chopped
1	stalk celery, chopped		salt and pepper
			mayonnaise

Mix all ingredients together and chill.

Potato Salad

8	medium potatoes, peeled, cubed and boiled until tender	1	tablespoon mustard
1½	cups salad dressing or mayonnaise	½	teaspoon salt
1	cup sour cream	¾	cup chopped celery
½	cup sweet relish	1	onion, chopped
1	tablespoon celery seed	1	cup fresh parsley
		4	hard-cooked eggs, chopped

Add all ingredients together. Add additional mayonnaise if needed. Chill in refrigerator.

Seven Layer Salad

1	10-ounce package frozen peas	1	cup chopped green pepper
1	head lettuce, shredded	4	slices bacon, fried crisp
1	cup chopped celery		Parmesan cheese
			mayonnaise

Cook peas as directed, cooking 1 minute only. Drain. Make layers of lettuce, celery, green pepper and peas. Spread a small amount of mayonnaise evenly over top and sprinkle with Parmesan cheese. Crumble bacon and sprinkle over top. Refrigerate overnight.

Wilted Lettuce Salad

4	slices bacon	1	tablespoon sugar
2	tablespoons vinegar		lettuce
4	tablespoons water		

Fry bacon until crisp. Remove and drain. To bacon drippings, add vinegar, water and sugar. Bring to a boil. Place lettuce in serving bowls. Pour liquid over lettuce and sprinkle bacon on top. Serves 2.

Wilted Spinach Salad

1	pound fresh spinach	1	teaspoon lemon juice
8	slices bacon	2	teaspoons sugar
½	cup sliced green onions	3	hard-cooked eggs,
2	tablespoons white wine		chopped
	vinegar		salt and pepper to taste

Remove stems from spinach and rinse well. Pat dry. Tear into bite-size pieces and place in a large bowl. Cook bacon until crisp; drain on paper towels. Crumble and set aside. Add onions, vinegar, lemon juice, sugar, salt and pepper to bacon drippings in pan; stir well and cook until bubbly. Immediately pour over spinach, tossing to coat well. Sprinkle with bacon and eggs. Serve immediately. Serves 6.

Macaroni Salad

1	12-ounce package shell macaroni, cooked	1½	cups mayonnaise
3	stalks celery, chopped	3	jalapeño peppers, chopped (optional)
1	whole green pepper, chopped		juice of 1 lemon
5	green onions, chopped		salt and pepper to taste

Cook macaroni, drain and add mayonnaise, lemon juice, salt and pepper. Let cool, then add remaining ingredients. Store in refrigerator.

Pope's Spicy Rice Salad

2	cups cooked rice, warm	¼	cup parsley
6	tablespoons olive oil	¼	cup chopped chives
3	tablespoons wine vinegar	½	cup cucumbers, cut into
1	teaspoon salt		small cubes
1	teaspoon black pepper	¼	cup chopped green onions
½	teaspoon tarragon	4	hard-cooked eggs
½	cup chopped green pepper	1	small jar pimento
¼	cup chopped celery		lettuce leaves

Mix cooked rice with olive oil, vinegar, salt, pepper and tarragon. Let stand to cool. Mix together green pepper, celery, parsley, chives, cucumber and chopped green onions. Add to rice. Place on lettuce leaves and garnish with hard-cooked eggs and pimento strips. Serves 4.

Chicken Salad

4	chicken breasts, cooked and deboned	½	cup softened cream cheese
1	cup chopped celery	2	tablespoons mayonnaise

Cut cooked chicken breasts into pieces. Add remaining ingredients. Add additional cream cheese if too dry. Chill in refrigerator.

☆

Shrimp Salad

1	quart cooked, peeled shrimp	1	teaspoon lemon pepper
3	cups cooked rice	1½	teaspoons mustard
½	cup cooking oil		juice of 1 lemon
1	clove crushed garlic	⅛	teaspoon red pepper

Mix cooked shrimp and cooked rice together. Mix remaining ingredients together and pour over shrimp and rice mixture. Chill in refrigerator.

Taco Salad

1	pound ground chuck	3	tomatoes, chopped
1	medium onion, chopped	4	ounces tortilla chips,
1	head lettuce, shredded		crumbled
1	cup grated Cheddar	2	avocados, sliced
	cheese		picante sauce

Lightly brown ground chuck and onion. Drain. Prepare salad with lettuce, cheese, tomatoes and tortilla chips. Top with avocados, meat and onion mixture. Add picante sauce over top. Serve.

Tuna Salad

1	9-ounce can tuna, flaked	1	stalk celery, chopped
2	sweet or dill pickles, diced	¼	cup mayonnaise or salad
2	hard-cooked eggs,		dressing
	chopped	1	apple, chopped (optional)

Combine all ingredients and serve on a lettuce leaf or make sandwiches.

Cherry Fluff

1	20-ounce can crushed	1	14-ounce can sweetened
	pineapple (drained)		condensed milk
1	21-ounce can cherry pie	1	cup chopped pecans
	filling	1	cup coconut (optional)
1	12-ounce carton whipped	1	7-ounce jar marshmallow
	topping		creme

Mix all ingredients together in a large bowl. Refrigerate.

Cranberry Congealed Salad

1	6-ounce package raspberry gelatin	2	16-ounce cans whole berry cranberry sauce
1	6-ounce package straw-berry gelatin	1	20-ounce can crushed pineapple, drained
3	cups boiling water	2	cups chopped pecans

Dissolve gelatin in boiling water. Stir in cranberry sauce with wire whisk. Chill in refrigerator until slightly thickened. Add pineapple and pecans. Pour into lightly oiled 9x13x2-inch baking dish. Chill 3 or 4 hours or overnight.

Five Cup Salad

1	cup coconut	1	cup miniature marshmallows
1	11-ounce can mandarin orange slices, drained and chopped	1	cup whipped cream
1	cup crushed pineapple, drained		

Mix all ingredients together. Chill in refrigerator.

Lewis's Lemon Gelatin Salad

1	6-ounce package lemon gelatin	1	egg, beaten well
3	cups hot water	½	cup sugar
1	cup miniature marshmallows	2	heaping tablespoons flour
3	bananas, sliced	1	16-ounce carton whipped topping
1	large can pineapple chunks, reserve juice	1	cup grated Cheddar cheese
		1	cup pecans, chopped fine

Mix gelatin with hot water. Add marshmallows. Cool in refrigerator. Add bananas and pineapple chunks. Pour into a 9x13-inch serving dish. Chill in refrigerator until firm. Mix pineapple juice, egg and sugar together. Cook over low heat until thick. Cool. Fold in whipped topping. Spread over gelatin mixture. Top with cheese and pecans. Refrigerate.

Orange Salad

1	3-ounce package orange gelatin	1	8-ounce can crushed pineapple
1¼	cups boiling water	1	8-ounce carton whipped topping
1	cup grated carrots		

Mix orange gelatin into boiling water. Add carrots and pineapple. Place in refrigerator. When slightly congealed, fold in whipped topping.

Pineapple Salad

1	6-ounce package lime gelatin	1	cup diced apples (do not peel)
2	cups hot water	1	cup chopped pecans
1	15½-ounce can pineapple tidbits		

Dissolve gelatin in 2 cups hot water. Drain syrup from pineapple and add enough water to make 2 cups. Add to gelatin. Chill in refrigerator until slightly thickened. Fold in pineapple, apples and pecans. Pour into salad mold or bowl and chill until firm.

Stained Glass Fruit Salad

1	can peach pie filling	2	cans mandarin oranges, drained
3	bananas, sliced		
1	package frozen strawberries, drained	2	small cans pineapple tidbits, drained

Drain all fruits except peach pie filling. Mix together and chill overnight. Serve in a clear glass bowl.

Rutledge's Strawberry Nut Salad

1	6-ounce package straw-berry gelatin	1	20-ounce can crushed pineapple
1	cup boiling water	3	medium bananas, mashed
2	10-ounce packages frozen strawberries, thawed	1	cup chopped pecans
		1	pint sour cream

Dissolve gelatin in boiling water. Fold in strawberries, pineapple, bananas and pecans. Pour one-half mixture into 12x8x2 baking dish. Chill in refrigerator until firm, about 2 hours. Spread sour cream over top. Gently spoon remaining mixture over top of sour cream. Chill overnight. Cut into squares to serve. Note: To speed up first step for mixture to jell, place in freezer about 20 minutes to set, then proceed.

Watergate Salad

1	20-ounce can crushed pineapple (drained)	2	cups whipped topping
2	cups chopped pecans	2	cups miniature marshmallows
1	6-ounce box pistachio instant pudding mix		

Mix all ingredients together and refrigerate.

Chicken and Dressing

Chicken:

1	3 to 4 pound chicken, cut up	1	stalk celery, cut in pieces
		1	stick oleo

Place chicken, celery and oleo in a Dutch oven. Cover with water and boil 45 minutes or until chicken is tender. Remove chicken and set aside. Reserve broth for dressing.

Dressing:

1	recipe baked cornbread (1 to 2 quarts crumbled cornbread)	1	bell pepper, chopped
		3	green onions, chopped
4	biscuits, crumbled or 4 slices bread, crumbled	2	teaspoons poultry seasoning
3	eggs	1	teaspoon sage
2	hard-cooked eggs	1	small jar pimientos, chopped
3	stalks celery, chopped		chicken broth

Mix all ingredients, except broth in a large bowl. Add enough broth to make a "soupy" mixture. Pour into a 9 x 13 inch baking dish. Place chicken pieces on top. Bake for 45 minutes in a 350 degree oven. Remove and serve hot.

☆
Cheesy Chicken Casserole

Helen Goodwin - Helen's Tea Room

1	5-pound hen or 2 fryers	1	cup tomato sauce
½	cup cooking oil	1	cup tomatoes (whole)
1	bell pepper, chopped	½	teaspoon comino seed
2	onions, diced fine	1	large bag noodles
2	garlic cloves, diced		grated Cheddar cheese
1	cup chopped celery		
1	small can chopped mushrooms		

Stew chicken and debone. Cook noodles in broth and drain. Sauté bell pepper, onions, garlic and celery in oil, but do not brown. Add mushrooms, tomatoes, tomato sauce, comino and chicken. Simmer until thick. Mix in noodles. Pour into casserole dishes. Sprinkle grated cheese on top. Bake in 400 degree oven 30 to 45 minutes until bubbly. Everyone calls this Aunt Helen's chicken that feeds a lot of people! Freezes well.

Chicken Ka-Bobs

Marinade:

½	cup Worcestershire sauce	2	tablespoons dry red wine
½	cup Italian dressing		(optional)
½	cup water	1	teaspoon season all
2	tablespoons brown sugar		

Mix marinade ingredients in a bowl; set aside.

Kabobs:

4	large boneless chicken breasts, cut in 2-inch cubes	2	large green peppers, cut in large cubes
4	ripe oranges, cut in cubes	1	red onion, cut in 1-inch cubes and separated
1	large can pineapple chunks, drained	8	firm cherry tomatoes
12	large mushrooms, cut in halves		

On foot long skewers, alternate the above ingredients. Dip in marinade and let sit for 1 hour. Start barbecue grill. Cook over medium heated grill until chicken is done, spooning marinade over skewers often.

☆

Robert's Spiced Glazed Chicken

1	cup apricot preserves	4	chicken breasts
½	cup Catalina dressing		salt and pepper to taste

Salt and pepper chicken breasts. Place in a baking dish. Mix preserves and dressing together. Pour over chicken. Bake in 375 degree oven for 1 hour, basting chicken every 15 minutes. This dish is delicious served over cooked rice.

Casey's Sweet and Sour Stir Fry Chicken

½	cup low sugar apricot spread	¼	cup cooking oil
1	tablespoon vinegar	½	pound small mushrooms
1	teaspoon garlic salt	2	large chicken breasts, skinned, deboned and cut in 1-inch pieces
1	teaspoon powdered ginger		
1	teaspoon soy sauce	1	6-ounce package frozen pea pods
⅛	teaspoon crushed red pepper	½	teaspoon salt
2	medium zucchini		

Stir apricot spread, vinegar, garlic salt, ginger, soy sauce and red pepper together until well blended. Set aside. Halve the zucchini lengthwise and cut in ¼-inch slices. Heat 2 tablespoons cooking oil in wok or 5 quart dutch oven until hot. Over high heat, cook zucchini and mushrooms with salt until zucchini is crisp-tender, stirring constantly. Transfer mixture to a platter. Add remaining oil to wok. Cook chicken until tender, stirring often. Add zucchini mixture and pea pods. Stir gently until heated. Add apricot spread mixture and stir gently until heated. Serve over cooked rice if desired. Makes 4 servings.

Southern Fried Chicken

1	2½ to 3 pound chicken - cut up	2	cups flour
		2	cups shortening
1	cup milk		salt and pepper to taste
1	egg, beaten well		

Rinse chicken well and drain. Sprinkle with salt and pepper. Mix egg and milk together. Place flour in a separate bowl. Melt shortening in frying pan over medium heat. Dip chicken into egg and milk mixture and then in flour. Place in frying pan. Do not crowd pieces. Cover and cook slowly 45 minutes to 1 hour. Turn 2 or 3 times during cooking period. For extra crispness, uncover frying pan during last 10 minutes of cooking period. Remove and drain on paper towels.

Easy Chicken and Dumplings

1	3 to 4 pound chicken, cut up	2	chicken bouillon cubes
4	stalks celery, chopped	2	to 3 cans (10 count) biscuits

Place chicken, celery and bouillon cubes in a large dutch oven. Cover with water. Bring to a boil and simmer 1 hour or until chicken is tender. Remove chicken and cool. Debone, cube and set aside. Place biscuits on floured surface. Kneading lightly, pat each biscuit to one-half inch thickness. Cut each biscuit into eight to ten pieces. Set aside. Bring broth to a boil and quickly drop cut biscuits into broth. Turn heat to low and cook 8 to 10 minutes. Add chicken to broth. Salt and pepper to taste.

Chicken and Rice

1	stick oleo	3	cups water
2	beef bouillon cubes	1½	cups uncooked rice
1	¼-ounce package dry onion soup mix	1	2½ to 3 pound fryer, cut up

Melt oleo in 9 x 13 inch baking dish. Add remaining ingredients except chicken and stir. Place chicken on top of mixture and bake in 350 degree oven for 1½ hours.

☆

Brown Bag Turkey

1	turkey, thawed	double strength grocery
	oil	bag
	salt and pepper	

Oil inside of grocery bag. Rub turkey with oil. Salt and pepper turkey. Place in bag and staple to close. Place bag inside a large broiler pan. Bake in 325 degree oven. For turkeys 12 pounds and under, bake 20 to 22 minutes per pound. For turkeys over 12 pounds, bake 10 to 18 minutes per pound. When turkey is done, remove from oven and punch holes in bottom of sack to drain juices into pan. When turkey is cool, remove and place on serving platter. Slice to serve.

Chicken Fried Steak

Steak:

1½	pounds tenderized round steak	2	cups flour
2	eggs, beaten		seasoned salt
1	cup milk		pepper
		2	cups shortening

Mix eggs and milk. Stir with fork until blended. Cut steak into serving pieces. Sprinkle with seasoned salt and pepper. Dip steak in flour, egg and milk mixture, then again in flour. Place shortening in frying pan and heat to medium heat. Grease is too hot if smoking. Place steak in frying pan, not crowding and cook 15 to 20 minutes turning every 5 minutes until steak is golden brown. Serve with gravy.

Gravy:

3	tablespoons flour	½	teaspoon salt
2	cups milk		dash of pepper

Remove ¼ cup melted shortening from frying pan that steak has been cooked in and place in another frying pan. Heat slowly. Add flour and stir with fork to make a smooth mixture. Brown slightly. Add milk, stirring constantly. Cook until thickened. Add salt and pepper. If gravy becomes too thick, slowly add more milk.

☆

Oven Barbecued Brisket

1	9 to 10 pound trimmed beef brisket	1	19-ounce bottle barbecue sauce
1	4-ounce bottle liquid smoke		lemon pepper

Sprinkle lemon pepper over brisket. Place in a large roasting pan. Pour liquid smoke over meat. Cover. (Use a large pan for brisket drippings) Place in 250 degree oven and bake 10 to 12 hours. Pour off grease. Cover with barbecue sauce and return to oven 1 hour uncovered. Remove and cool to slice.

Texas Goulash

2 pounds round steak - cubed
¼ cup shortening
½ cup chopped onion
1 green bell pepper - chopped

2 teaspoons paprika
2 teaspoons salt
1 28-ounce can whole or stewed tomatoes
¼ cup water
2 tablespoons flour

Brown meat in shortening. Add onion and bell pepper. Cook about 15 minutes or until vegetables are tender. Add seasonings and tomatoes. Simmer at low heat on top of stove 2 to 2½ hours or in 350 degree oven 1 hour until meat is tender. Blend flour and water until smooth. Stir into mixture and bring to a boil, stirring constantly. Delicious served over rice.

Spicy Tomato Steak

1½ pounds tenderized round steak, cut into small pieces
1 teaspoon garlic salt
1 teaspoon pepper
½ cup flour
1 large onion, chopped fine
1 green bell pepper, chopped fine
3 stalks celery, chopped fine

1 8-ounce can tomato sauce
½ 10-ounce can tomatoes and chilies
1 teaspoon chili powder
1 teaspoon Worcestershire sauce
½ cup cooking oil to brown steak in

Salt and pepper steak. Dredge in flour and place in hot oil. Brown on both sides; drain on paper towels. Combine remaining ingredients together. Place steak in a baking dish and pour tomato mixture over steak. Bake in 350 degree oven for 1 hour or until meat is tender. Add a little water if sauce becomes too thick. This dish is hot!

Brower's Barbecued Meatballs

Meatballs:

2	eggs, slightly beaten	1	teaspoon salt
1	pound ground beef	1	cup oats or soft bread
1	pound bulk sausage		crumbs

Combine all ingredients together. Mix well. Shape into small balls. Place on baking sheet and bake in 375 degree oven for 20 minutes. Drain. This makes about 15 small meatballs.

Barbecue Sauce:

½	cup catsup	½	teaspoon Worcestershire
⅓	cup chopped onion	1	tablespoon lemon juice
2	tablespoons green onion	½	teaspoon mustard
¼	cup chopped celery	¼	cup water
2	tablespoons brown sugar	1	tablespoon cooking oil
1	tablespoon vinegar		

Sauté onions and celery in cooking oil. Add remaining ingredients and simmer 10 minutes. Add meatballs and simmer another 5 minutes. Serve.

☆

Mom's Meat Loaf

1½	pounds ground beef	2	8-ounce cans tomato
2	eggs		sauce
1	teaspoon salt	1	cup barbecue sauce
1	teaspoon pepper	3	tablespoons brown sugar
1	green bell pepper, chopped	1	cup cooking oats or 2
1	stalk celery, chopped		slices bread, crumbled
1	small onion, chopped		

Mix tomato sauce, barbecue sauce and brown sugar together. Set aside. Mix remaining ingredients together. Add ⅓ sauce mixture to meat mixture. Form two loaves and place in a greased casserole dish. Pour ½ of remaining sauce over loaves and bake at 375 degrees for 1 hour. Pour remaining sauce over loaves and bake an additional 15 minutes. Remove from oven.

Lasagne

1½	pounds ground beef	1	10-ounce package shredded Swiss cheese
1	onion, chopped		
1	28-ounce can tomatoes	1	10-ounce package cheddar cheese
1	14-ounce jar pizza sauce		
1	teaspoon oregano leaves	½	cup Parmesan cheese
1	teaspoon parsley flakes	1	8-ounce package lasagne noodles, cooked
1	teaspoon basil		
1	teaspoon chili powder		salt and pepper to taste
1	10-ounce package shredded mozzarella cheese		Parmesan cheese to sprinkle on cooked lasagne

Lightly brown meat and onion. Salt and pepper to taste. Add tomatoes, pizza sauce and seasonings. Simmer 30 minutes, stirring occasionally. Boil lasagne noodles according to package directions. Rinse and cool. In a 9 x 13 inch baking dish, layer ½ of the noodles, sauce and cheeses. Repeat layer. Bake in 400 degree oven for 30 minutes or until bubbly. Remove and sprinkle with Parmesan cheese. For easy serving, let stand for 20 minutes before cutting.

Michael's Sizzleburgers

1½	pounds ground chuck	grated cheese
	salt, pepper, seasoning salt and Worcestershire	

Form 4 patties. Sprinkle with salt, pepper and seasoning salt. Have skillet hot. Sear meat on each side to lock in juices. Reduce heat and cook 10 to 15 more minutes or until done. Add dash of Worcestershire while cooking. Sprinkle with grated cheese last 2 minutes and melt. Place on your choice of hamburger buns and top with pickles, onions, lettuce and tomatoes.

One Dish Savory Spaghetti

1	pound ground beef	1	14½-ounce can tomatoes
¼	pound pan sausage	1	teaspoon salt
	(optional)	1	teaspoon Worcestershire
1	small onion, chopped		sauce
1	8-ounce can tomato sauce	1	tablespoon brown sugar
2	cups water	1	teaspoon oregano
1	teaspoon pepper	2	stalks celery, chopped
6	drops hot pepper sauce	4	ounces spaghetti (do not
1	teaspoon chili powder		exceed this amount)
1	bell pepper, chopped		

Lightly brown beef and sausage. Add remaining ingredients, including uncooked spaghetti. Cook over low heat for 45 minutes.

☆

Stuffed Bell Peppers

6	medium bell peppers	1	pound ground beef
2	tablespoons chopped	1	teaspoon salt
	onion	1	cup soft bread crumbs
1	teaspoon pepper	1	10¾-ounce can tomato
1	egg, slightly beaten		soup

Cut tops off peppers and remove stems and seeds. Rinse peppers and drain. Combine meat, onion, salt, pepper, bread crumbs, egg and ½ can of soup. Mix well and stuff peppers with this mixture. Place in a frying pan that has 1 to 1½ inches boiling water. Cover with a tight lid and slowly cook 30 minutes or until peppers are tender. Drain. Heat remaining soup and pour over peppers.

Deep Dish Pizza

1	16-ounce package hot roll mix	1	14½-ounce can stewed tomatoes, drained and mashed
1	pound sausage or ground meat, cooked and drained	1	small onion, chopped
2	6-ounce packages mozzarella cheese	1	bell pepper, chopped

Mix crust according to package directions for pizza crust. Place in a deep dish. Mix cooked meat, tomatoes, pepper and onion together and simmer on low heat for 15 minutes. Alternate layers of cheese and meat mixture on crust, topping with cheese. Bake in a 400 degree oven 20 to 30 minutes to melt cheese and brown crust.

Smothered Liver

1	pound beef liver, thinly sliced	¼	cup flour
6	slices bacon	½	cup hot water
3	onions, thinly sliced		salt and pepper

Fry bacon until crisp. Set aside. Slowly fry onion slices in bacon drippings until tender. Remove and set aside. Salt and pepper liver and coat with flour. Sauté liver in bacon drippings. Brown two minutes on each side. Pour onions on top. Add hot water. Crumble bacon and pour on top of onions. Cover and cook for 2 more minutes. Serves four.

Corn Dogs

1½	cups pancake mix	10	wieners
½	cup cornmeal		sticks for wieners
2	tablespoons sugar		oil for frying
1	cup milk		

Mix first four ingredients together. Insert sticks into wieners. Dip wieners in batter. Deep fry in hot oil until golden brown.

Chicken Enchiladas

24	corn tortillas	1	10¾-ounce cream of
1	3 to 4 pound chicken, cut		mushroom soup
	up	1	10-ounce can tomatoes
1	stalk celery, cut in half		and chilies
1	onion, chopped	1	pound grated Cheddar
1	bell pepper, chopped		cheese
1½	teaspoons chili powder	2	tablespoons oleo
1	10¾-ounce cream of		
	chicken soup		

Place chicken and celery in Dutch oven. Cover with water and boil on medium heat for 1 hour or until chicken is tender. Remove chicken and debone. Reserve broth. Sauté onion and bell pepper in oleo. Add ½ cup chicken broth, chili powder, soups and tomatoes and chilies. Stir. Add deboned chicken. Bring remaining chicken broth to a boil and dip each tortilla into broth to soften. In a 13 x 9 x 2 inch casserole dish, make alternate layers of tortillas, chicken mixture and top with Cheddar cheese. Bake in 350 degree oven for 30 to 45 minutes.

Tacos

1	pound ground beef	1	cup water
1	small onion, chopped	8	crispy taco shells
1	clove garlic, chopped	2	tomatoes, chopped
½	teaspoon cumin	1	head lettuce, shredded
1	teaspoon salt	1	cup grated Cheddar
1	teaspoon pepper		cheese

Lightly brown ground beef, onion and garlic. Add cumin, salt and pepper. Add 1 cup water and simmer for 10 minutes. Drain. Heat taco shells in oven. To prepare tacos: Place meat in shell. Top with lettuce, tomatoes and sprinkle with cheese.

Tamale Pie

24	tamales	1	large onion, chopped fine
1	24-ounce can chili	2	cups grated Cheddar
1	8-ounce can tomato sauce		cheese

Combine chili and tomato sauce. Combine onion and Cheddar cheese. Place 12 tamales in a large baking dish. Pour one half of the sauce over tamales. Sprinkle ½ of the onion and cheese mixture over sauce. Repeat layer. Bake in 350 degree oven about 20 minutes or until bubbly. Serves 8.

Frito Pie

3	cups corn chips	1	to 2 cups grated cheese
½	chopped onion	1	19-ounce can chili

Place 2 cups corn chips in baking dish. Sprinkle onion and half of cheese over chips. Pour chili over onion and cheese. Top with remaining corn chips and cheese. Bake 15 to 20 minutes at 375 degrees until bubbly. Serves four.

Fajitas For Two

	flour tortillas	1	cup Italian Dressing
1	pound skirt steak, trimmed and tenderized		

Cut steak into strips and marinate in dressing 4 hours or overnight. Grill over hot charcoal or "sizzle fry" in a hot frying pan with a tablespoon of melted shortening. When using frying pan method: After cooking for a few minutes, drain liquid and continue cooking until meat is tender. Serve in a warm flour tortilla with sautéed green peppers and onions. Top with pico de gallo. Warm tortilla by placing in a hot dry frying pan, turning quickly to heat but not brown. May also heat in microwave.

Sautéed Peppers and Onions:

2	tablespoons margarine	2	green onions, chopped tops and bottoms
1	small green bell pepper, cut in rings		

Melt margarine in a small frying pan. Add pepper and onion. Cook until onions are clear and soft.

Pico De Gallo:

½	cup onions, chopped fine	1	teaspoon cilantro, fresh, coarsely chopped (optional)
¼	cup chopped jalapeño peppers		
½	cup tomatoes, chopped	¼	teaspoon salt
1	tablespoon vinegar		

Mix all ingredients together.

Huevos Rancheros

Sauce:

1	tablespoon cooking oil	½	cup canned green chilies, with juice (chopped)
½	onion, chopped	½	teaspoon cumin
1	bell pepper, chopped		salt and pepper to taste
2	cups canned tomatoes, with juice		

Sauté onions and bell pepper in oil until onions are transparent. Add tomatoes and green chiles. Add salt, pepper and cumin. Simmer 15 to 20 minutes.

Filling:

4	eggs, scrambled or fried - set aside	4	corn tortillas oil for frying
1	cup grated cheese		

Heat oil in frying pan. Dip each tortilla in oil for a few seconds to soften. Drain on paper towels. Place egg on tortilla. Top with sauce and grated cheese.

☆

Roundup Chili

2	pounds coarse ground meat (beef, turkey or venison)	1	teaspoon paprika
		1	teaspoon cumin
1	onion, chopped fine	1	teaspoon oregano
2	cloves garlic, chopped fine	½	cup chili powder
1	tablespoon salt	¼	cup flour
1	teaspoon pepper (red or black)	1	8-ounce can tomato sauce
		2	cups water

Sear ground meat until lightly brown. Add flour and stir to cover meat. Place meat in a large saucepan. Add remaining ingredients and simmer over low heat for 1 hour or until meat is tender. Add additional water if mixture becomes too thick. Serve hot.

☆

Tortilla Dogs

10	wieners	10	thick corn tortillas
5	slices cheese		cooking oil

Slice the wieners lengthwise and halfway through. Cut cheese in half and place inside each wiener. Wrap tortillas around wiener and secure with a toothpick. Heat oil in frying pan. Place tortilla in hot oil and fry until tortilla is crisp. Serve hot.

Baked Pork Chops

6	pork chops	½	cup finely diced celery
½	teaspoon salt	2	tablespoons brown sugar
⅛	teaspoon pepper	1	teaspoon prepared
2	8-ounce cans tomato		mustard
	sauce		juice of half of lemon
½	cup water	2	tablespoons oil

Sprinkle chops with salt and pepper. Brown in hot oil. Remove and place in a shallow greased baking dish. Combine remaining ingredients and pour over chops. Cover and bake in 350 degree oven 1 hour or until chops are tender.

☆

Oven Spareribs

4	pounds spareribs, pork	½	teaspoon garlic salt
1	6-ounce can (⅔ cup) orange or lemonade juice concentrate	½	cup honey

Place ribs, meaty side down in a shallow roasting pan. Bake at 450 degrees for 30 minutes. Drain off fat; turn ribs and bake 30 more minutes. Drain off fat. Combine remaining ingredients, brush on ribs. Reduce temperature to 350 degrees, cover pan and bake one hour or until tender, brushing with sauce occasionally.

Fried Fish Fillets

2	pounds fish fillets, cut in small pieces	1	teaspoon salt
1	cup flour	1	teaspoon black pepper
1	cup yellow cornmeal		oil for frying

Rinse fish and drain on paper towels. Mix flour, cornmeal, salt and pepper in a small brown paper bag. Heat oil to 365 degrees. Drop a few pieces at a time into bag, shake to coat fish, remove and drop in hot oil. Cook until golden brown. Drain on paper towels.

☆

Broiled Flounder

Flounder:

2	large flounder	1	lemon, sliced thin

Score flounder and place lemon slices in the slits. Place in a baking dish.

Sauce:

1	stick oleo, melted	2	green onions, with tops - diced
2	teaspoons poultry seasoning		juice of 1 lemon
1	tablespoon parsley		salt and pepper

Mix all ingredients together. Place flounder under broiler and cook 20 to 30 minutes, basting with sauce until fish is done.

☆

Fried Oysters

1	cup cornmeal	2	12-ounce containers fresh oysters, drained
1	cup flour		salt and pepper
2	eggs		oil for frying
3	tablespoons milk		
2	teaspoons Chesapeake Bay style seafood seasoning		

Sprinkle salt, pepper and seafood seasoning over oysters. Combine cornmeal and flour together. Mix eggs and milk together. Stir slightly. Dip oysters in egg mixture and dredge in flour mixture. Pour oil to a depth of 2 inches in a large frying pan. Heat to 375 degrees. Fry oysters in oil, turning once, until golden brown. Drain on paper towels. Serves 6.

Salmon Patties

1	15-ounce can salmon	½	cup flour
1	whole egg		oil for frying
1	teaspoon baking powder		

Pour off juice from salmon and set aside. Stir egg into salmon. Add flour and stir. Add baking powder to ¼ cup of the salmon juice. Mixture will foam. After foaming, add to salmon mixture. Mixture will be thin. Drop by teaspoons in hot oil. Brown lightly on both sides. Drain on paper towels.

Michael's Shrimp Creole

1	cup chopped onion	1	14-ounce can tomatoes
1	cup chopped celery	2	tablespoons brown sugar
1	cup chopped bell pepper	1	clove garlic - minced
3	tablespoons cooking oil	1	bay leaf
1½	teaspoons salt	2	cups water
1	tablespoon flour		dash of Worcestershire
2	teaspoons chili powder		sauce
½	teaspoon hot pepper sauce	1	quart fresh shrimp, shelled
1	12-ounce can tomato paste		and deveined
1	8-ounce can tomato sauce		

Sauté onion, celery and bell pepper in cooking oil. Add remaining ingredients except shrimp. Cook slowly in electric skillet or heavy saucepan over low heat for 1½ hours, stirring occasionally. Add more water if needed. Remove bay leaf. Add shrimp; cook 30 minutes more. Serve over cooked rice. Prepare rice for 4 to 6 according to package directions.

Carl's Boiled Shrimp

3	pounds fresh shrimp	½	cup vinegar
1	teaspoon salt		
2	teaspoons seafood seasoning		

Remove heads from shrimp. Place shrimp, salt, seafood seasoning and vinegar in a large saucepan. Cover shrimp with water. Bring to a boil. Reduce heat, cover and continue boiling for 10 minutes. Remove from heat. Drain. Chill in refrigerator.

M. B.'s Shrimp Gumbo

1	quart shrimp - peeled and deveined	1	bell pepper, chopped
1	10½-ounce can white crabmeat	1	cup chopped celery
2	cups frozen cut okra	3	cloves minced garlic
1	18¾-ounce can tomatoes	3	tablespoons bacon drippings
1	10-ounce can tomatoes and chilies	1	heaping teaspoon seafood seasoning
1	onion, chopped		salt and pepper to taste
		3	cups water

Combine tomatoes and 3 cups water. Add onions, celery, bell pepper and garlic. Boil until tender. Add bacon drippings, crabmeat, shrimp, okra, seafood seasoning, salt and pepper. Bring to a boil. Lower heat and simmer 10 to 15 minutes. Serve over cooked rice. Serves 6 to 8.

Kolterman's Shrimp Remoulade

(from a Cajun friend)

Remoulade Sauce:

2	yolks of hard-cooked eggs, sieved	3	tablespoons Worcestershire sauce
3	tablespoons yellow prepared mustard	4	tablespoons wine vinegar
3	cloves garlic, minced	4	tablespoons dried parsley flakes
3	cups mayonnaise		dash of hot pepper sauce
3	tablespoons horseradish		salt and pepper to taste
2	tablespoons paprika		

Blend all sauce ingredients together and chill in refrigerator. May be stored in refrigerator for a week. This dressing is also great with crabmeat or served as a dressing on a green salad.

4	pounds fresh shrimp, boiled, cleaned and chilled

To serve, shred lettuce and place on individual salad plates. Mound shrimp over lettuce. Use Remoulade Sauce for your dressing. Delicious!!!

Lemon-Butter Broiled Shrimp

2	pounds large fresh shrimp, peeled and deveined	¼	cup lemon juice
		2	cloves garlic, minced
2	sticks (1 cup) butter or margarine, melted	½	teaspoon salt
		¼	teaspoon pepper

Sauté garlic in butter until tender; remove from heat and stir in lemon juice, salt and pepper. Arrange shrimp in a single layer in a shallow baking pan; pour butter sauce over shrimp. Place under broiler and broil 6 inches from heat for 5 to 6 minutes or until shrimp are done, basting once with sauce. Yields: 4 to 6 servings.

Famous Fried Shrimp

2	pounds shrimp, shelled and deveined	1	teaspoon pepper
		1	egg
2	teaspoons seafood seasoning - Chesapeake Bay style	1½	cups milk
			cracker meal
			flour
1	teaspoon salt		cooking oil

Shell and devein shrimp. Sprinkle with seafood seasoning, salt and pepper. Place egg and milk in a bowl and beat slightly. Set aside. Place cracker meal and flour in separate bowls. Dip each shrimp in the following order; flour, egg and milk mixture and last in cracker meal. Place in hot oil and fry 2 or 3 minutes or until golden brown. Drain on paper towels. To prepare ahead of time: After coating shrimp, place on waxed paper, making layers and store in refrigerator until ready to fry.

Galveston Beer Batter Shrimp

2	pounds shrimp, shelled and deveined or 1½ pounds peeled, deveined frozen shrimp	1	teaspoon seafood seasoning - Chesapeake Bay style - optional
1	12-ounce can beer	1	cup flour
1	teaspoon salt		flour to dip shrimp in

Shell and devein shrimp. If using frozen shrimp, thaw and drain on paper towels. Combine salt, seafood seasoning and flour in mixing bowl. Gradually beat in beer until batter is thin. Dip shrimp first in more flour, then in beer batter. Deep fry in hot oil 2 to 3 minutes until golden brown.

Baked Dove

12	doves, dressed	½	cup celery
1	10½-ounce can condensed	1	cup dry vermouth
	cream of mushroom soup	1	cup water
1	envelope dry onion soup		
	mix		

Preheat oven to 350 degrees. Place doves in a 2 quart casserole. Combine remaining ingredients and pour over the doves. Cover and bake for 2 to 3 hours, turning and basting frequently.

☆

Baked Wild Duck

any number of wild ducks,	charcoal
dressed	2 pounds hickory chips,
salt and pepper to taste	soaked in water
dry red wine	

Place charcoal at one end of grill. Start fire and let burn until gray. Place the hickory chips over the coals. Salt and pepper ducks. Place them on grill at opposite end of coals. Place lid down on grill and smoke the ducks 30 to 45 minutes. Remove and roll each duck in foil, adding 2 ounces of wine per duck. Bake in 275 degree oven, breast side down for 3 hours. Remove and serve.

☆

Wild Turkey

1	wild turkey	1	cup chopped celery
1	onion, chopped	1	stick oleo, melted
1	bell pepper, chopped		salt and pepper

Wash turkey and wipe dry. Pour oleo over bird. Salt and pepper outside and inside cavity. Fill the cavity with onions, bell pepper and celery. Place in a large roaster and bake in 450 degree oven as follows:

7 to 9 pounds 2 to 2½ hours
10 to 13 pounds 2½ to 3 hours
14 to 17 pounds 2½ to 3¼ hours
18 to 21 pounds 3¼ to 3½ hours

Remove lid about 30 minutes prior to end of baking time to brown.

Braised Quail

4	quail, dressed	1	cup red wine
1	stick oleo	6	tablespoons currant jelly

Melt oleo in skillet. Sauté quail in oleo until lightly browned. Bring red wine to a boil and add to oleo. Cover and cook 6 to 10 minutes, turning quail 3 to 4 times during cooking. Remove quail. Add jelly to wine sauce. Mix well. Bring to a boil, stirring constantly. Return quail to pan and coat well with glaze. Remove quail to serving plates and spoon glaze over quail.

Fried Frog Legs

6	large frog legs	½	cup flour
1	teaspoon salt	2	eggs
1	teaspoon pepper	½	cup milk
½	cup cornmeal		cooking oil for frying

Pour cooking oil in deep skillet or fryer to a depth of 2 to 3 inches. Sprinkle frog legs with salt and pepper. Mix cornmeal and flour together. Mix eggs and milk together. Dip frog legs in flour and meal mixture, then in egg and milk mixture and again in flour and meal mixture. Deep fry, turning for even browning and crispness. Remove when done and drain on paper towels.

☆

Squirrel Stew

4	young squirrels	3	tablespoons flour
2	onions, chopped	1	tablespoon chopped
2	cups diced carrots		parsley
6	potatoes, cubed		salt and pepper
½	cup chopped celery		bay leaf

Dress and cut up squirrels. Salt and pepper to taste. Place in a large pot with onions, bay leaf and celery. Cover with cold water and simmer for 2 hours. Add potatoes and carrots. Cook until tender. Mix flour with a small amount of hot water to make a paste. Slowly add to stew to thicken. Add parsley.

Venison Roast

4 to 5	pound venison roast	2	green onions, chopped
1½	cups wine vinegar	4	tablespoons vegetable oil
1½	cups dry wine		garlic salt
½	cup flour		pepper

Mix wine, vinegar and enough water to cover roast. Soak in refrigerator overnight. Remove and rinse. Salt and pepper roast and dredge in flour. Heat oil in roasting pan and brown roast. Sprinkle green onions on top and add 2 cups water around sides of roast. Cover and cook in 350 degree oven approximately 3 hours or until tender.

☆

Barbecue Venison

1	3-pound venison roast	1	teaspoon chili powder
1	medium onion, chopped	1½	cups water
1	cup celery, chopped	4	tablespoons lemon juice
2	tablespoons vinegar	1½	teaspoons liquid smoke
2	tablespoons brown sugar	¼	teaspoon oregano
1	cup catsup	2	bay leaves
3	tablespoons Worcestershire sauce	2	garlic cloves, crushed
			salt and pepper to taste

Place meat in roaster. Mix remaining ingredients and pour over meat. Bake, tightly covered at 275 degrees for 5 to 6 hours or until meat will shred. Serve on toasted buns. Serves 15 to 20.

New Year's Eve Black-Eyed Peas

2	(10-ounce) packages frozen black-eyed peas	1	10-ounce can tomatoes and chilies
¼	cup chopped jalapeño peppers (mild)	1	teaspoon salt
1	small onion, chopped	1	teaspoon pepper
4	tablespoons bacon drippings	1	teaspoon chili powder

Cook peas according to package directions. Add remaining ingredients and cook 10 more minutes. Serve with hot cornbread.

Easy Baked Beans

1	23 ounce can pork and beans	½	onion, chopped
		1	cup barbecue sauce
½	green bell pepper, chopped	½	cup brown sugar
1	tablespoon mustard	3	slices bacon (optional)

Mix all ingredients together except bacon and pour into baking dish. Place bacon on top and bake in 400 degree oven 30 to 45 minutes until sugar turns firm around edge of dish.

Red Beans and Rice

1	pound package dried pinto beans	2	teaspoons salt
		1	teaspoon pepper
2	cloves garlic, minced		ham hock, salt pork or 3
1	medium onion, chopped		slices bacon to season
¼	teaspoon sugar		cooked rice

Rinse beans well. Place in a large pot or Dutch oven. Cover well with water. Add remaining ingredients except rice and cook on low heat until done, approximately 3 hours. Do not let water boil too low. Add boiling water to beans as they cook. For a thicker soup, mash a few cooked beans with a fork and mix into broth. Serve over cooked rice. Link sausage may also be added to beans the last 30 minutes of cooking time.

Chili Beans

1	pound dry pinto beans	1	medium onion, chopped
3	cups water	3	teaspoons chili powder
½	pound salt pork or 4 slices bacon	1	teaspoon salt
		1	teaspoon pepper
1	clove garlic, minced	2	teaspoons sugar

Rinse beans. Place in a large saucepan and add water to cover beans well. Bring to boil. Add remaining ingredients. Cover and cook on low heat for 3 hours or until tender. Add additional boiling water if needed. Mash about 10 beans with a fork to make soup broth thick. Add additional salt if needed.

Hall's Bacon Wrapped Green Beans

3	16 ounce cans whole green beans	1	cup brown sugar
		1	stick oleo, melted
1	pound sliced bacon	2-3	dashes soy sauce

Mix brown sugar, oleo and soy sauce together. Pour into a 9 x 13 casserole dish. Cut each slice of bacon into 3 pieces. Wrap a piece of bacon around 5 or 6 green beans. Secure with a toothpick and place over soy sauce mixture. Cover and refrigerate overnight. Bake in 350 degree oven for 20 minutes. Remove and place under broiler to brown bacon. Serve.

Broccoli-Rice Casserole

½	cup chopped celery	1	10¾ ounce can cream of chicken soup
½	cup chopped onion		
4	tablespoons butter	1	10¾ ounce can cream of mushroom soup
2	10 ounce packages frozen chopped broccoli		
1	cup cooked rice	1	pound pasteurized process cheese spread, cubed

Sauté celery and onion in butter. Prepare broccoli according to package directions; drain. Combine all ingredients in a large bowl and mix well. Pour into a large buttered casserole dish and sprinkle with topping. Bake in 350 degree oven for 30 minutes or until bubbly.

Topping:

3	tablespoons oleo	2	slices bread, crumbled

Melt oleo and stir in bread crumbs to coat well.

Skillet Cabbage

4	cups shredded cabbage	¼	cup vinegar
1	bell pepper, shredded	¼	cup bacon drippings
1	cup diced celery	2	teaspoons sugar
1	large onion, sliced	1	teaspoon salt
2	tomatoes, chopped, optional	1	teaspoon pepper

Combine all ingredients in a large skillet. Cook over medium heat for 20 to 30 minutes. Yields: 6 servings.

Glazed Carrots

| 1 | pound carrots, peeled and thinly sliced | 3 | tablespoons brown sugar |
| 4 | tablespoons butter | 2 | teaspoons ginger |

Cook carrots in a small amount of boiling water about 10 minutes or until crisp-tender. Drain, reserving 2 tablespoons liquid. Combine 2 tablespoons liquid with butter, brown sugar and ginger. Heat thoroughly. Add carrots, stirring gently and cook another 3 to 4 minutes.

Skillet Corn

2	17 ounce cans corn, drained	8	slices bacon, chopped
2	green onions, chopped	1	teaspoon sugar
1	green bell pepper, chopped	½	teaspoon salt
		½	teaspoon pepper

Sauté bacon until lightly brown. Remove and set aside. Sauté onions and bell pepper in bacon grease. Add remaining ingredients and simmer for 10 minutes. Sprinkle bacon on top.

Duke's Corn and Rice Casserole

2	17 ounce cans cream style corn	⅛	teaspoon salt
1	cup minute rice	½	teaspoon pepper
1	egg, slightly beaten	⅛	teaspoon ground nutmeg

Mix all ingredients together in a large bowl. Pour into a lightly greased 2 quart baking dish. Bake in 375 degree oven for 25 minutes. Serves 6.

Corn Bake

4	ears fresh corn	1	green onion and top,
2	eggs, beaten		chopped (optional)
1	cup milk	1	teaspoon sugar
3	tablespoons butter		
½	green bell pepper, chopped (optional)		

Cut corn from cobs and scrape ears. Combine all ingredients in buttered 1½ quart casserole. Bake at 350 degrees for 45 minutes. Serves 6.

Fried Eggplant

1	pound eggplant	½	cup grated Parmesan
2	teaspoons lemon and pepper seasoning salt		cheese
1	cup yellow cornmeal		oil for frying

Peel eggplant. Cut into ¾ x 3 inch strips. Pat dry on paper towels. Sprinkle with lemon and pepper seasoning salt. Dredge in cornmeal. Fry in hot oil until golden brown. Remove and drain on paper towels. Sprinkle with Parmesan cheese. Yields: 4 to 6 servings.

Macaroni and Cheese

1	7 ounce package elbow macaroni	2	cups cubed pasteurized process cheese spread or
2	tablespoons oleo		Cheddar cheese
½	cup milk		salt and pepper to taste

Cook macaroni according to package directions. Drain. Add oleo, milk, cheese, salt and pepper. Stir over low heat until cheese is melted. To prevent macaroni from boiling over - butter pot 2 inches down from the top.

Cheesy Spaghetti

1	8 ounce package thin spaghetti, cooked and drained	8	ounces Cheddar cheese, grated
8	ounces pasteurized process cheese spread, grated	1½	cups milk
		1½	sticks butter

Add milk, butter and one half of the cheeses to cooked spaghetti. Place over low heat and stir until cheese is melted. Pour into a buttered baking dish and sprinkle remaining cheeses over top. Bake in a 350 degree oven, 15 to 20 minutes until bubbly.

Okra And Tomatoes

1	stick oleo	1	28 ounce can tomatoes
1	small onion, chopped fine	⅛	teaspoon sugar
3	cups cut okra		salt and pepper to taste

Sauté onion and okra in oleo until tender. Add remaining ingredients. Cook over low heat an additional 20 minutes.

Buffet Potatoes

1	2 pound package frozen hash brown potatoes, partially thawed	1	10¾ ounce can condensed cream of chicken soup
½	cup oleo, melted	1	cup sour cream
¼	cup chopped onion	2	cups shredded Cheddar cheese

Mix all ingredients together and pour into 13 x 9 x 2 casserole dish. Sprinkle with topping and bake in 350 degree oven for 1 hour.

Topping:

3	cups corn flakes, coarsely crushed	1	stick oleo, melted

Mix together to coat corn flakes.

Stuffed Baked Potatoes

4	potatoes, baked	1	cup shredded cheese
6	tablespoons milk		paprika, salt and pepper
4	tablespoons butter		chopped fresh parsley

Cut baked potatoes in half lengthwise. Scoop potatoes out of skin leaving shell intact. Mash potato with milk and butter. Stir in cheese, salt and pepper. Refill potato shells with mixture. Reheat in oven. Remove and sprinkle with paprika and garnish with parsley. Makes 8 servings.

Cheezy Potatoes

6	medium size new potatoes (red)	1	8 ounce carton sour cream
1	pound pasteurized process cheese spread	1	stick oleo, melted
			salt and pepper

Rinse and scrub potatoes well. Do not peel. Cut into ¼ inch slices. Place in a large saucepan and cover with water. Cook 20 to 30 minutes until slightly tender. Drain. Place half of potatoes in a 9 x 13 inch baking dish. Salt and pepper. Spread half of sour cream and half of melted oleo over top of potatoes. Slice half of cheese on top. Repeat layer. Bake in 450 degree oven approximately 20 minutes or until bubbly.

☆

SPO's Spanish Rice

1	cup rice	1	tablespoon chili powder
½	bell pepper, chopped	1	teaspoon salt
1	green onion, chopped	1	teaspoon pepper
1	carrot, diced	2	tablespoons cooking oil
1	small can English peas (optional)	¼	teaspoon cumin
1	10 ounce can tomatoes and chilies	1	clove garlic, minced
		1	cup water

Sauté rice, bell pepper, onion and carrot in oil until rice is brown. Add remaining ingredients. Cover and cook 15 to 20 minutes or until liquid is absorbed. Serves 6.

Baked Spinach

6	slices bacon	1	¼ ounce envelope onion
2	10 ounce packages frozen		soup mix
	chopped spinach, thawed	½	cup grated Parmesan
	and well drained		cheese
1½	cups commercial sour		
	cream		

Fry bacon until crisp, drain on paper towels. Combine spinach, sour cream and soup mix. Stir well. Spoon into a lightly greased 1 quart casserole. Sprinkle cheese over mixture. Bake 350 degrees for 30 minutes. Crumble bacon and sprinkle over top. Yields: 6 servings.

☆

Nanny's Baked Squash

3	pounds yellow squash	½	stick oleo
½	cup chopped onion	1	tablespoon sugar
2	eggs		salt and pepper

Wash and cut up squash. Place in a saucepan and add 1 cup water. Cover and boil until tender. Drain thoroughly and mash with a fork. Add remaining ingredients. Pour into a buttered baking dish. Sprinkle crumb mixture over top. Bake in a 375 degree oven for approximately 1 hour or until slightly brown.

Crumb Mixture:

½	stick oleo, melted	¼	cup cracker meal or bread
			crumbs

Mix together and sprinkle over top of squash.

☆

Squash Fritters

1	10 ounce package frozen	½	cup cracker crumbs
	sliced yellow squash	1	tablespoon oil
2	eggs beaten	½	teaspoon salt
2	green onions, chopped fine	½	teaspoon pepper
½	green bell pepper, chopped		
	fine		

Cook squash according to package directions. Drain and mash. Mix squash with remaining ingredients. Drop by tablespoon into hot oil and fry until golden brown. Drain on paper towels.

Sweet Potato Casserole

Mixture 1:

3	cups mashed sweet potatoes (may use canned)	½	stick oleo, melted
1	cup sugar	½	cup milk
½	teaspoon salt	1	teaspoon vanilla
3	eggs	2	teaspoons cinnamon

Mix all ingredients together and place in a buttered 9 x 13 casserole dish.

Mixture 2:

1½	cups brown sugar, packed	1	stick oleo, melted
1	cup flour	1	cup chopped nuts
½	teaspoon baking powder		

Mix together and pour over Mixture 1. Cook in 350 degree oven 30 to 40 minutes or until brown.

☆

Broiled Tomatoes

5	large ripe tomatoes	1	teaspoon dried oregano
2	cups French bread crumbs, crushed	1	teaspoon basil
½	stick oleo, melted	½	teaspoon salt
1	clove garlic, minced	1	teaspoon pepper
2	green onions and tops, minced		

Rinse tomatoes. Cut tops off and scoop out the pulp. Discard pulp. Combine remaining ingredients and fill tomato shells. Bake in 350 degree oven for about 20 minutes. Place under broiler until golden brown. Sprinkle with Parmesan cheese if desired.

Granny's Turnip Greens

2	pounds fresh turnip greens	2	tablespoons bacon
6	slices bacon		drippings
4	cups water	1	teaspoon sugar
1	tablespoon white vinegar	1	teaspoon salt
3	green onions, chopped	1	teaspoon pepper

Thoroughly rinse turnip greens under cool water. Tear into bite-size pieces. Mix all ingredients in a Dutch oven and bring to a boil. Cover, reduce heat and simmer for 1 hour. Note: One 16 ounce package of frozen turnip greens can be substituted for fresh turnip greens.

☆

Vegetable Medley

1	bell pepper, chopped	3	cups tomatoes, peeled and
½	medium onion, chopped		chopped
½	stick oleo	1	teaspoon sugar
2	cups fresh okra	1	teaspoon lemon and
2	cups fresh corn, (cut from cob)		pepper seasoning salt

Sauté bell pepper and onion in oleo until tender. Add remaining ingredients. Cook over low heat 20 to 30 minutes until corn is tender.

☆

Lemon-Butter Zucchini

2	medium zucchini	2	tablespoons lemon juice
½	stick oleo, melted		Parmesan cheese

Rinse zucchini and drain. Cut in half crosswise and cut each piece lengthwise into 6 sticks. Place zucchini in a steaming rack over boiling water. Cover and steam for 6 minutes or until crisp-tender. Place in a serving dish. Mix lemon juice and oleo together. Pour over zucchini and toss gently to cover. Sprinkle with Parmesan cheese. Serves 4

Steven's Angel Biscuits

5	cups all-purpose flour	3	tablespoons sugar
3	tablespoons baking powder	1	cup shortening
		1	package dry yeast
1	teaspoon baking soda	½	cup warm water
1	teaspoon salt	2	cups buttermilk, heated

Dissolve yeast in warm water. Sift flour, baking powder, soda, salt and sugar together. Cut in shortening. Add yeast mixture with warm buttermilk and add to flour mixture. Stir quickly until flour is moistened. Turn onto a lightly floured board and knead for 2 minutes. Store in an airtight container in refrigerator. Will last up to 1 week. Use as needed. Roll dough out on a floured board and cut with biscuit cutter. Bake on a greased cookie sheet in 450 degree oven for 10 to 12 minutes.

Cheezy Biscuits

2	cups flour	¼	cup shortening
2½	teaspoons baking powder	1	cup shredded sharp
½	teaspoon salt		Cheddar cheese (4 ounces)
½	teaspoon red pepper	1	cup buttermilk

Combine first four ingredients. Cut shortening in with a fork. Add cheese. Dough will be coarse. Add buttermilk. Drop dough by heaping teaspoonfuls about 2 inches apart on greased baking sheet. Bake in 450 degree oven 10 to 12 minutes. Yields about 3 dozen biscuits.

Drop Biscuits

1¼	cups self-rising flour	2	tablespoons sugar
1	cup whipping cream (not whipped)		

Combine ingredients and stir until blended. Drop biscuits by the teaspoon onto lightly greased baking sheets. Bake at 425 degrees 8 to 10 minutes.

Country Biscuits

2	cups flour	1	tablespoon baking powder
½	teaspoon salt	5	tablespoons shortening
1	teaspoon sugar	1	cup buttermilk
¼	teaspoon soda		

Sift together dry ingredients. With a fork, cut in shortening until coarse. Add buttermilk and stir until mixed. Turn out on a floured board and knead ½ minute. Roll ⅜ inch thick. Cut with a biscuit cutter or a small glass dipped in flour. Place on ungreased cookie sheet. Bake in 450 degree oven 12 to 15 minutes until golden brown. Makes about 2 dozen.

Beer Bread

3	cups self-rising flour	1	12 ounce can beer
3	tablespoons sugar		

Mix flour and sugar together. Add beer and mix just until blended. Pour into greased 9 x 5 x 3 inch loaf pan. Let rise 10 minutes. Bake at 350 degrees for 40 to 50 minutes. Brush top with butter while hot.

Iron Skillet Cornbread

1	teaspoon soda	1	teaspoon baking powder
1½	cups buttermilk	¼	cup sugar
1	egg, beaten	½	teaspoon salt
1	cup cornmeal	2	tablespoons oil
1	cup flour		

Mix together buttermilk, egg and soda. Add cornmeal, flour, baking powder, sugar, salt and oil. Stir until mixed well. Pour into greased hot cast iron 10 inch skillet. Bake in 425 degree oven for 20 to 30 minutes or until golden brown. For crunchy edges, place oil in iron skillet. Place over heat until oil is hot. Pour cornbread batter into hot oil. Bake as directed.

Jalapeño Cornbread

1½	cups cornbread mix	1	cup cream style corn
2	eggs	1	medium onion, chopped
1	cup milk	¼	cup chopped jalapeño
¼	cup cooking oil		peppers
2	tablespoons sugar	1	2-ounce jar chopped
1	cup grated Cheddar cheese		pimiento

Mix all ingredients together and pour into a greased 9 x 13 inch pan. Bake at 350 degrees 30 to 45 minutes until brown.

Hush Puppies

2	cups cornmeal	½	teaspoon sugar
1	cup flour	2	eggs
2	tablespoons baking powder	1	small onion, chopped fine
1	teaspoon salt		sweet milk
			oil for frying

Mix all ingredients together and add enough sweet milk to make a soft dough. Drop by spoonfuls into hot oil and fry until golden brown.

Six Week Muffins

1	15 ounce box raisin bran cereal	3	cups sugar
1	cup melted shortening	1	quart buttermilk
4	eggs, beaten	5	teaspoons soda
5	cups flour	2	teaspoons salt

Mix raisin bran, flour, soda, salt and sugar in a large mixing bowl. Add beaten eggs, shortening and buttermilk. Mix well. Store in covered container in the refrigerator and use as desired. When ready to use, do not stir. Fill greased muffin pans ¾ full and bake in 400 degree oven 15 to 20 minutes.

French Toast

2	eggs	1	teaspoon sugar
¼	cup milk		bread slices
¼	teaspoon salt		

Beat eggs until frothy. Add milk, salt and sugar. Mix well. Dip bread slices in mixture and place in a buttered frying pan. Cook until golden brown. Serve with butter, powdered or granulated sugar. Also good with syrup.

Favorite Pancakes

1¼	cups sifted flour	1	egg, beaten
1	tablespoon baking powder	1	cup milk
¼	teaspoon salt	2	tablespoons cooking oil
1	tablespoon sugar		

Mix dry ingredients together in mixing bowl. Combine egg, milk and oil and add to dry ingredients. Stir slightly. Pour onto ungreased griddle or non-stick frying pan. Turn when bubbles appear and pop on top of uncooked side of pancake. Cook until knife inserted comes out clean. Serve hot with melted butter, syrup or honey.

Velvety Waffles

3	eggs, separated	½	teaspoon salt
1¾	cups milk	2	cups sifted flour
½	cup cooking oil	1	teaspoon sugar
4	teaspoons baking powder		

Separate eggs and beat yolks until light and fluffy. Stir in milk and add cooking oil. Mix dry ingredients together. Stir in milk and oil mixture. Beat egg whites well and fold into mixture. Pour small amounts onto hot waffle iron and cook until brown.

Hall's Sopaipillas of Dallas

2	packages dry yeast	3	tablespoons melted
2	cups warm water		shortening or cooking oil
¼	cup sugar	2	teaspoons salt
1	egg	5	cups flour

Cinnamon - Sugar Mixture:

1	cup sugar	1	teaspoon cinnamon

Dissolve yeast in ½ cup of the warm water. Add 2 teaspoons of the sugar. Mix and set aside for 5 minutes. Beat egg. Add oil and remaining sugar. Stir slightly. Add to yeast mixture. Mix flour and salt together and add to yeast mixture. Add remaining water. Mix well. Place dough on a well floured surface and knead 3 to 5 minutes. Place in a greased bowl and let rise 45 minutes to 1 hour. Divide dough and roll out on a floured surface. Roll to pie crust thickness. Cut into squares or triangle shapes. Let rise 10 minutes. Fry in hot oil, turning to lightly brown both sides. Drain on paper towels. Dip in cinnamon - sugar mixture. Serve with butter and honey. Delicious!!

Homemade Flour Tortillas

6	cups flour	1	to 1½ cups warm water
1	heaping teaspoon baking powder	2	tablespoons salt
		¾	cup shortening

Combine dry ingredients and add shortening, then warm water until well blended, but not too sticky. Turn out onto floured surface and knead for about 3 minutes. Pinch off biscuit size balls and roll out evenly in thin circles on floured surface. Cook on hot griddle until lightly browned. Serve warm. Makes 2 dozen.

One Hour Rolls

(Easy and Delicious!)

2	envelopes dry yeast	½	cup melted shortening or
½	cup warm water		oil
1½	cups buttermilk, heated to	1	teaspoon salt
	lukewarm	3½	cups sifted flour
¼	cup sugar	½	teaspoon baking soda

Dissolve yeast in warm water. Combine warm buttermilk, sugar and melted shortening. Sift flour, salt and soda into large bowl. Mix yeast with milk mixture and add to flour mixture. Mix well. Let stand 10 minutes. Roll out onto floured surface and cut or shape into desired roll and place in buttered baking dish. Let stand 30 to 45 minutes and bake at 425 degrees 20 to 30 minutes until light brown.

Doggones

(Because they are so doggone good!)

1	10 - count can biscuits	1	cup shortening

Remove biscuits from can. Place on waxed paper and cut each biscuit into 4 pieces. Heat shortening in skillet. Drop biscuit pieces into hot oil - do not crowd. Cook about 30 seconds on each side or until golden brown. Remove and place on paper towels to drain.

Dip in your choice of :
    sugar   powdered sugar
    sugar and cinnamon -
    1 cup sugar mixed with
    1 teaspoon cinnamon

Serve warm.

Cinnamon Breakfast Ring

3	10 count cans biscuits	1	cup brown sugar
½	cup granulated sugar	2	teaspoons water
1	tablespoon cinnamon	1	cup nuts
1	stick oleo		

Sprinkle nuts in bottom of bundt cake pan. Mix granulated sugar and cinnamon together. Quarter biscuits and roll in sugar and cinnamon mixture. Place biscuits over nuts. Melt oleo, brown sugar, and water together and boil for two minutes. Pour over biscuits. Bake in 350 degree oven for 25 minutes.

☆

Banana Nut Bread

½	cup oleo	1	teaspoon vanilla
1½	cups sugar	1	cup mashed bananas (3 to
2	eggs		4 bananas)
1½	cups flour	1	teaspoon soda
4	tablespoons buttermilk	½	cup chopped pecans

Cream oleo and sugar together. Add eggs and mix well. Mix flour and soda together . Add to oleo, sugar and egg mixture. Add remaining ingredients and mix well. Pour into a greased and floured 3 x 5 x 9 inch loaf pan. Bake in 350 degree oven for 1 hour or until wooden pick inserted in center comes out clean. Cool in pan for 10 minutes. Remove and spread icing over top and let drizzle down sides.

Icing:

1	pound box powdered sugar	2	tablespoons milk
1	stick oleo, melted	1	teaspoon vanilla

Mix all ingredients together and stir until well blended. Pour over cake.

Spicy Pumpkin Bread

2¾	cups sugar	1	teaspoon cloves
1	cup cooking oil	1	teaspoon nutmeg
3	eggs	1	teaspoon allspice
1	16 - ounce can pumpkin	1	teaspoon cinnamon
3½	cups flour	1	teaspoon salt
½	teaspoon baking powder	1	cup chopped pecans
1	teaspoon soda		

Cream sugar, oil and eggs together. Add pumpkin. Stir until mixed. Let stand for 5 minutes. Sift dry ingredients together and add to pumpkin mixture. Stir in pecans. Fill 3 - 1 pound coffee cans (greased and floured) ½ full. Bake in 325 degree oven 1 hour and 15 minutes or until done. Remove from oven. Cool 5 minutes. Remove from cans.

Strawberry Bread

3	cups flour	4	eggs, well beaten
2	cups sugar	2	10 - ounce packages
1	teaspoon baking soda		frozen strawberries,
2	teaspoons cinnamon		thawed *Reserve ½ cup
1	teaspoon salt		juice for spread.
1	cup cooking oil		

Mix all ingredients together. Stir well until blended. Pour into 2 - 4 x 8 inch greased and floured loaf pans. Bake at 350 degrees for 1 hour or until done. Remove and cool. Slice bread into thin slices. Spread with cream cheese spread and top with another slice to make a "sandwich". Cut to desired sizes. Serve.

Cream Cheese Spread:

1	8 - ounce package cream cheese, softened		* remaining ½ cup strawberry juice

Mix together, using enough strawberry juice to make a spreadable mixture.

Grandma's Gingerbread

1	cup molasses	2	cups flour
2	teaspoons soda	½	cup sugar
2	eggs	1	cup milk
½	teaspoon ginger	1	teaspoon cinnamon
½	cup shortening		

Mix shortening, sugar and eggs. Add remaining ingredients. Bake in greased and floured 9 x 13 inch pan 375 degrees for 30 minutes.

Fresh Apple Cake

2	cups sugar	¼	teaspoon nutmeg
1	cup shortening or oleo	¼	teaspoon allspice
2	eggs	1	cup chopped pecans
½	cup water	1	tablespoon cocoa
1	teaspoon soda	1	teaspoon vanilla
2½	cups flour	3	apples, peeled and cut up
1	teaspoon cinnamon		fine
1	teaspoon salt		

Dissolve soda in water. Cream sugar and shortening. Add eggs to creamed mixture. Add spices, cocoa and salt to flour. Gradually add flour and soda-water mixture to creamed mixture. Beat well. Add apples and pecans. Stir in vanilla. Mix well. Bake in a greased and floured tube pan in 350 degree oven 60 to 70 minutes. Remove from oven. Cool 5 to 10 minutes and remove from pan.

Icing:

1	cup brown sugar	1	stick oleo
¼	cup milk		

Mix all ingredients together in a saucepan and bring to a boil. Boil exactly 3 minutes. Pour over cake.

☆

Easy Fruit Cake

½	pound candied pineapple, chopped	4	cups chopped pecans
		1½	cups coconut
½	pound candied cherries, chopped	½	cup flour
		2	14 ounce cans condensed
1	pound dates, chopped		milk

Mix fruit and pecans together. Add coconut, flour and milk. Mix well and pour into greased and floured tube pan. Cover with heavy brown paper to bake. Bake in 350 degree oven for 1 hour. Remove from oven and cool for 15 minutes. Remove from pan.

Banana Cake

1½	cups sugar	1	teaspoon baking powder
½	cup butter or shortening	4	bananas, mashed
2	eggs, separated	1	teaspoon vanilla
½	cup buttermilk	2½	cups all-purpose flour
1	teaspoon soda		sifted 3 times

Cream sugar and shortening or butter. Add egg yolks and beat thoroughly. Add milk, soda, baking powder and bananas. Add flour, egg whites (not beaten) and vanilla. Mix and pour into three well greased and floured 9" cake pans. Bake at 350 degrees for about 25 minutes. Cool in pans 10 minutes. Remove and ice with butter icing, spreading generously between layers as well as the outside.

Butter Icing:

2	cups sugar	1	cup milk
1	cup butter	1	teaspoon vanilla

Place first three ingredients in heavy saucepan and boil until mixture forms a soft ball when dropped from a teaspoon into cold water. Remove from heat. Add vanilla. Beat until thick and creamy.

Banana Split Cake

Mix together and pat into bottom of 9 x 12 pan:

1	stick oleo, melted	2	cups graham cracker crumbs

Mix together and beat until fluffy:

2	cups powdered sugar	2	eggs
2	sticks oleo		

Pour over top of cracker crumb mixture. Layer the following on top of mixture:

5	bananas sliced - sprinkle with Fruit Fresh to keep from turning brown	1	12 ounce carton whipped topping
1	20 ounce can crushed pineapple, drained	1	cup chopped pecans

Refrigerate 3 to 4 hours or overnight.

☆

Carrot Cake

1½	cups cooking oil	2	cups flour
4	eggs	3	cups grated carrots
2	cups sugar	1	teaspoon soda
1	teaspoon salt	2	teaspoons cinnamon

Mix sugar, eggs and cooking oil. Add carrots and mix well. Add dry ingredients that have been sifted together. Bake at 325 degrees for 30 minutes in 2 greased and floured 8 inch cake pans.

Icing:

1	8 ounce package cream cheese	1	teaspoon vanilla
1	stick butter, melted	1	cup chopped nuts
		1	pound box powdered sugar

Mix well and spread over cake.

K.P.'s Chocolate Cake

2	cups flour	3	tablespoons cocoa
2	cups sugar	2	eggs, well beaten
2	teaspoons cinnamon	1	teaspoon soda
½	teaspoon salt	½	cup buttermilk
2	sticks oleo	1	teaspoon vanilla
1	cup water		

Mix flour, sugar, cinnamon and salt together. Set aside. Place oleo, water, and cocoa in a saucepan. Bring to a boil. Pour over flour mixture. Mix eggs, soda, buttermilk and vanilla together and add to batter. Mix well. Pour into a greased and floured 15½ x 10½ x 1 inch pan. Bake in 350 degree oven 20 to 25 minutes. Start icing the last 5 minutes cake is baking.

Icing:

1	stick oleo	1	cup chopped pecans
3	tablespoons cocoa	1	teaspoon vanilla
6	tablespoons milk		
1	16 ounce box powdered sugar		

Mix oleo, cocoa and milk in a saucepan. Place over low heat and stir until oleo is melted. Do not boil. Remove and add powdered sugar, pecans and vanilla. Mix well. Spread over cake as soon as removed from oven.

☆

Turtle Cake

1   box German chocolate cake mix

Prepare as directed. Pour ½ of the batter in a 9 x 13 greased and floured pan and bake 20 minutes at 350 degrees. While cake is baking, melt in double boiler:

1	pound caramels	1	stick oleo
1	cup evaporated milk		

Pour over cooked cake. Sprinkle the following over caramel mixture:

12	ounces milk chocolate chips	1	cup chopped pecans

Pour remaining batter over top and bake approximately 20 more minutes at 350 degrees.

Texas Fudge Cake

Rich and Delicious!

Cake:

½	cup cocoa	2	sticks oleo, melted
2	cups sugar	4	eggs
1½	cups flour	1	cup chopped pecans

Mix cocoa, sugar and flour together. Add oleo and eggs. Beat well. Add pecans. Pour into a greased 9 x 13 pan. Bake in 350 degree oven for 25 minutes. Remove from oven.

Icing:

1	7 ounce jar marshmallow creme	⅓	cup milk
1	stick oleo, melted	1	teaspoon vanilla
½	cup cocoa	1	box powdered sugar

Spread marshmallow creme over top of warm cake. Mix remaining ingredients together and stir to mix well. Spread over marshmallow creme.

☆

Chocolate Chip Pound Cake

1	cup butter	2	teaspoons vanilla extract
2	cups sugar (reserve ½ cup and set aside)	1	12 ounce package semi-sweet chocolate morsels
6	eggs, separated	1	4 ounce package sweet baking chocolate, grated
3	cups flour		
½	teaspoon salt	1	cup sifted powdered sugar
¼	teaspoon baking soda	1	tablespoon milk
1	8 ounce carton sour cream		

Cream butter and 1½ cups sugar together until light and fluffy. Add yolks, 1 at a time beating well after each addition. Mix flour, salt and soda together. Add to creamed mixture alternately with sour cream. Stir in vanilla, 1½ cups chocolate morsels and grated chocolate. Beat egg whites until frothy. Gradually add remaining ½ cup sugar to egg whites a small amount at a time, beating until stiff peaks form. Fold egg whites into batter. Pour batter into a greased and floured 10 inch tube pan. Bake at 325 degrees for 1 hour and 20 to 25 minutes. Cool in pan for 10 to 15 minutes. Invert onto a serving plate. Combine powdered sugar and 1 tablespoon milk, stirring well. Add more milk for a thinner glaze. Spoon over warm cake. Sprinkle remaining chocolate morsels over glaze. Cool.

Mocha Brownie Pound Cake

1	cup butter or oleo	3	cups flour
½	cup shortening	½	cup cocoa
3	cups sugar	1	cup milk
5	eggs	1	cup chopped pecans

Cream butter, shortening and sugar together. Add eggs, 1 at a time. Blend in flour, cocoa and milk. Mix well and pour in a greased and floured tube pan. Sprinkle with pecans. Place in a cold oven. Bake at 300 degrees for 2 hours. Remove from oven. Cool 10 to 15 minutes. Remove from pan.

☆

German Chocolate Cake

1	4 ounce package German chocolate	2½	cups sifted flour
		1	teaspoon vanilla
½	cup boiling water	½	teaspoon salt
1	cup oleo	1	teaspoon soda
2	cups sugar	1	cup buttermilk
4	egg yolks, unbeaten	4	egg whites, stiffly beaten

Mix chocolate in boiling water. Cool. Cream oleo and sugar until fluffy. Add egg yolks, one at a time. Beat well. Add melted chocolate and vanilla. Mix. Sift together salt, soda, and flour. Add alternately to mixture with buttermilk. Beat until smooth. Fold in egg whites. Pour into three greased and floured 8 inch cake pans. Bake at 350 degrees for 30 to 40 minutes. Cool and remove from pans.

Frosting:
Combine in a saucepan:

1	cup evaporated milk	¼	pound (1 stick) oleo
1	cup sugar	1	teaspoon vanilla
3	egg yolks		

Cook and stir over medium heat until thick, about 12 minutes.

Add:

1⅓	cups coconut	1	cup chopped pecans

Mix well and spread layers, sides and top of cake.

Coconut Pound Cake

5	eggs	½	teaspoon salt
2	cups sugar	½	cup milk
1	cup cooking oil	1	teaspoon vanilla
2	cups flour	1	teaspoon coconut extract
1½	teaspoons baking powder	1	cup coconut

Beat together eggs and sugar. Add remaining ingredients. Bake in greased and floured tube pan in 350 degree oven for 1 hour. Let cool in pan while making glaze.

Glaze:

1	cup sugar	¼	cup oleo
½	cup water	1	teaspoon coconut extract

Mix in saucepan and boil for 1 minute. While cake is still in pan, pour glaze slowly around and on top of cake. Let cool for about 30 minutes. Remove. Wrap in foil to keep moist.

Cream Cheese Pound Cake

2	sticks oleo	3	cups sugar
1	stick butter	3	cups flour
1	8 ounce package cream cheese, softened	6	eggs
		3	teaspoons vanilla

Cream oleo, butter, cream cheese and sugar. Gradually add flour and eggs, alternately. Mix well. Stir in vanilla. Pour into a large greased and floured tube pan. Place in a cold oven. Bake at 300 degrees 1½ to 2 hours or until done. Remove and cool.

Italian Crème Cake

1	cup buttermilk	5	eggs, separated
1	teaspoon soda	2	cups flour
2	cups sugar	1	teaspoon vanilla
1	stick oleo	1	cup chopped pecans
½	cup shortening	1	cup coconut

Preheat oven to 325 degrees. Combine soda and buttermilk. Set aside. Cream sugar, oleo and shortening. Add egg yolks, one at a time. Beat well after each addition. Add buttermilk and soda alternately with flour to the creamed mixture. Stir in vanilla. Beat egg whites until stiff. Fold into batter. Gently fold in pecans and coconut. Bake in 3 greased and floured 9 inch cake pans for 25 - 30 minutes.

Cream Cheese Icing:

1	8 ounce package cream cheese, softened	1	16 ounce box powdered sugar
1	stick oleo, softened	1	teaspoon vanilla

Cream the cheese and oleo. Add vanilla. Slowly beat in powdered sugar. Spread between cake layers and outside of cake. To decorate cake, arrange pecan halves on top.

☆

Lemon Loaf Cake

1	cup butter	2	cups sifted flour
1¾	cups sugar	1	tablespoon lemon extract
6	eggs		

Cream butter and sugar thoroughly. Add eggs, one at a time. Blend thoroughly after each addition. Gradually add flour and extract. Bake in a 10 inch greased and floured tube cake pan for approximately 1 hour at 325 degrees. Remove from oven.

Oatmeal Cake

1½	cups boiling water	½	teaspoon salt
1	cup quick cooking oats	1	cup brown sugar
1	stick oleo	1	cup granulated sugar
1⅓	cups flour	2	eggs
1	teaspoon cinnamon	1	cup chopped dates
1	teaspoon soda		

Pour boiling water over oats. Let cool. Cream oleo and sugars together. Add eggs. Mix together flour, cinnamon, soda and salt. Add to creamed mixture. Add oats and dates. Mix well. Pour into a greased and floured 9 x 13 oblong pan. Bake in 350 degree oven about 35 minutes.

Topping:

1	cup chopped pecans	1	cup brown sugar
1	cup coconut	¼	cup milk
⅔	cup oleo		

Mix all ingredients together in a saucepan. Bring to a boil. Pour over cake. Place cake under broiler. Toast pecans and coconut. Remove from broiler.

Mandarin Orange Cake

1	box butter cake mix	3	eggs
1	cup cooking oil		
1	11 ounce can mandarin oranges, plus juice		

Mix all ingredients together. Pour into a greased and floured 13 x 9 x 2 inch cake pan. Bake in a 350 degree oven for 30 to 40 minutes. Remove and cool.

Icing:

1	9 ounce carton whipped topping	1	3 ounce package instant vanilla pudding
1	8 ounce can crushed pineapple		

Mix together and spread over cake. Refrigerate.

Orange Pound Cake

1½	cups butter or margarine, softened	¼	teaspoon salt
3	cups sugar	¾	cup plus 2 tablespoons milk
5	eggs	¼	cup orange juice
3½	cups flour	1	teaspoon vanilla extract
1	teaspoon cream of tartar	3	tablespoons grated orange rind
2	teaspoons baking powder		

Cream butter; gradually add sugar, beating until light and fluffy. Add eggs, one at a time, beating after each addition. Combine flour, cream of tartar, baking powder and salt. Add to creamed mixture alternately with milk and orange juice. Mix until blended. Stir in vanilla and orange rind. Pour batter into a greased and floured 10 inch tube pan. Bake at 325 degrees for 1 hour and 30 minutes or until a wooden pick inserted in center comes out clean. Cool for 10 minutes. Remove from pan.

Picken's Texas Pecan Cake

3	cups sugar	1	pound candied cherries, chopped
1	pound oleo, softened		
7	eggs, separated	5	cups flour
2	ounces lemon extract	1	teaspoon soda
4	tablespoons wine or grape juice	4	cups pecans, chopped
1	pound candied pineapple, chopped		

Separate eggs. Beat whites until frothy and set aside. Beat yolks. Set aside. Heat wine and mix with 1 teaspoon soda. Set aside. Mix pecans with 2 cups flour to coat well. Set aside.Cream sugar and oleo together. Add egg yolks and lemon extract. Beat well. Add remaining 3 cups flour and mix well. Add wine and soda mixture. Add pineapple, cherries and flour coated pecans. Fold in beaten egg whites. Bake in four greased loaf pans in 250 degree oven for 2 hours. (Test for doneness with toothpick.) Remove from oven. Loosen around edges of pan with a knife. Cool completely in pan. Remove and wrap in foil.

Punch Bowl Cake

1   2 layer size package yellow
    cake mix, prepared
    according to directions,
    cooked and crumbled.
2   21 ounce cans cherry pie
    filling
2   4 serving size packages
    instant pudding, vanilla or
    chocolate prepared
    according to package
    directions

2   8½ ounce cans crushed
    pineapple
4   bananas, sliced
1   8 or 9 ounce carton frozen
    whipped topping, thawed
1½ cups chopped pecans
1½ cups shredded coconut

Use a large, clear bowl. Crumble half of cake into bottom of bowl. Top with a layer of cherry pie filling, then layers of pudding, pineapple, sliced bananas, whipped topping, pecans and coconut. Repeat layers. Save a few cherries, pecans and pineapple to garnish top if desired. Chill.

Better Than Sex Cake

1   yellow cake mix
1   20 ounce can crushed
    pineapple
1   cup sugar
3   bananas, sliced
1   6 ounce package vanilla
    instant pudding mix

3   cups milk
1   8 ounce carton whipped
    topping
1   cup chopped pecans

Prepare yellow cake mix according to package directions. Bake in 9 x 13 greased and floured pan. Cool. Punch holes in top with a fork. Mix pineapple and sugar together in a saucepan. Place over low heat and cook until mixture slightly thickens. Remove and cool. Spread over cake. Place bananas over top. Mix pudding mix and milk together until slightly thick. Spread over bananas. Spread whipped topping over bananas. Sprinkle pecans over topping. Refrigerate overnight.

Hummingbird Cake

3	cups flour	1	cup crushed pineapple
1	teaspoon soda		with juice (8-ounce can)
½	teaspoon salt	3	medium bananas, chopped
2	teaspoons cinnamon	1½	cups chopped pecans or
2	cups sugar		walnuts
1½	cups cooking oil	2	teaspoons vanilla
3	eggs		

Combine flour, sugar, salt, soda and cinnamon in a large mixing bowl. Add eggs and oil, stirring until dry ingredients are moistened. Do not beat. Stir in vanilla, pineapple, pecans and bananas. Pour into a greased and floured tube pan. Bake in 350 degree oven for 1 hour and 5 minutes. Cool in pan. Remove.

Cream Cheese Frosting:

1	8-ounce package cream cheese, softened	1	teaspoon vanilla
½	cup butter or margarine, softened	1	cup chopped pecans
		1	cup coconut
2	cups powdered sugar (or one 16-ounce box)		

Combine cream cheese and butter. Cream until smooth. Add powdered sugar and beat until fluffy. Stir in vanilla. Spread on top and side of cake. Sprinkle pecans and coconut on top.

☆

Mexican Wedding Cake

2	cups flour	1	20-ounce can crushed
2	cups sugar		pineapple and juice
2	teaspoons baking soda	1	banana, mashed (optional)
½	teaspoon salt	1	cup chopped pecans
2	eggs		

Mix all ingredients together. Blend well. Pour into a 9 x 13 inch greased and floured pan. Bake at 350 degrees approximately 40 minutes or until done.

Frosting:

1	stick oleo, softened	2	teaspoons vanilla
1	8-ounce package cream cheese, softened	2	tablespoons milk
		1	cup chopped pecans
2	cups powdered sugar		(optional)

Mix well and spread over warm cake.

Pineapple Upside Down Cake

1	box yellow cake mix	1	cup brown sugar
1	stick margarine	1	cup chopped pecans
1	20-ounce can pineapple slices, drained maraschino cherries		

Melt 1 stick margarine in a large cast iron skillet or oblong 9 x 13 baking dish. Press brown sugar over top. Place pineapple slices on top of sugar. Place cherry in center of pineapple. Sprinkle pecans over top. Mix yellow cake mix according to directions and pour batter over top. Bake in 350 degree oven for 45 minutes or until done. Cool and remove from pan.

Red Velvet Cake

½	cup shortening	½	teaspoon salt
1½	cups sugar	1	teaspoon vanilla
2	eggs	1	teaspoon soda
2	ounces red food coloring	1	cup buttermilk
2	tablespoons cocoa	1	tablespoon vinegar
2½	cups flour		

Cream shortening and sugar. Add eggs and beat. Mix flour, salt and soda together. Set aside. Mix coloring with cocoa. Add vinegar and mix well. Add to egg mixture. Add flour mixture alternately with buttermilk to creamed mixture. Add vanilla and beat well. Pour into two 8-inch greased and floured pans and bake in 350 degree oven for 30 minutes. Baked layers may be split to make four.

Frosting:

3	tablespoons flour	1	cup milk
1	cup butter, softened	1	cup sugar
1	teaspoon vanilla		

Cook flour and milk together in a saucepan over low heat until thick. Cool. Cream sugar, butter and vanilla until fluffy. Add to flour and milk mixture. Beat until mixture has the consistency of whipped cream. Spread on layers. Sprinkle with coconut or nuts if desired.

Strawberry Cake

1	package white cake mix	⅔	cup salad oil
1	small box (4 serving size)	4	eggs
	strawberry gelatin	½	10-ounce package frozen
½	cup water		strawberries, thawed

Mix all ingredients in mixing bowl and beat with an electric mixer 3 to 5 minutes until blended. Bake in a greased and floured 13 x 9 x 2 inch pan in 350 degree oven for 30 to 40 minutes.

Icing:

1	box (2 cups) powdered sugar	½	10-ounce package straw-berries
¾	stick margarine, softened or melted		

Soften or melt margarine. Add powdered sugar, strawberries and juice and mix well. Spread over top of cake.

Wine Cake

1	18½-ounce box yellow cake mix	½	cup water
		¾	cup sherry wine
1	6-ounce package instant vanilla pudding mix	½	cup cooking oil
		1	teaspoon ground nutmeg
4	eggs		

Combine all ingredients in order given and beat for 5 minutes. Pour into greased and floured tube pan. Bake in preheated 350 degree oven for 45 minutes. Remove from pan. Prepare glaze and pour over warm cake.

Glaze:
1½ cups powdered sugar   wine

Add a few drops of wine to powdered sugar and stir.

Favorite Cupcakes

White Cupcakes:

2	cups sifted flour		⅔	cup milk
1⅓	cups sugar		2	teaspoons vanilla
2½	teaspoons baking powder		2	eggs
½	teaspoon salt		¼	cup milk
½	cup shortening			

Sift dry ingredients into mixing bowl. Add the shortening, ⅔ cup milk and vanilla; beat on low speed for 2 minutes. Add eggs and ¼ cup milk. Place cupcake liners in cupcake pans. Fill ⅓ full. Bake in 350 degree oven approximately 15 minutes. Remove and cool. Makes 24 cupcakes.

Chocolate Cupcakes:

1¾	cups flour		½	cup shortening
1⅓	cups sugar		1	cup buttermilk
1	teaspoon soda		1	teaspoon vanilla
½	teaspoon salt		2	eggs
6	tablespoons cocoa			

Sift dry ingredients in mixing bowl. Add shortening, buttermilk and vanilla. Beat 2 minutes at medium speed. Add eggs and beat 2 more minutes. Fill cupcake liners ⅓ full. Bake 350 degrees approximately 15 minutes. Remove and cool. Makes approximately 24 cupcakes.

Icing:

2	cups (1 box) powdered sugar, sifted		4	to 6 tablespoons milk, heated
½	stick oleo, melted		1	teaspoon vanilla

Add melted oleo to sifted powdered sugar. Slowly add heated milk, 1 tablespoon at a time until desired spreading consistency. Add vanilla. Spread over top of cupcakes. For chocolate icing: Add 3 tablespoons cocoa to melted oleo and mix well.

☆

Overnight Coffee Cake

1	12-count package frozen yeast rolls	1	cup brown sugar
		1	teaspoon cinnamon
½	3-ounce package butterscotch pudding mix	1	stick butter
		1	cup chopped pecans

Grease bundt pan. Place rolls in pan. Sprinkle pudding mix over rolls. Melt butter. Mix butter with brown sugar and cinnamon. Pour over rolls. Sprinkle pecans over cinnamon mixture. Cover with a cloth and let rise overnight at room temperature. Bake in 350 degree oven 20 to 30 minutes.

☆

Sour Cream Coffee Cake

6	tablespoons brown sugar	1	cup sour cream
1	cup pecans	2	eggs
2	sticks butter or margarine, softened	2	cups flour
		1	teaspoon baking powder
1	teaspoon vanilla	2	cups sugar

Mix brown sugar and pecans; set aside. Cream butter and sugar together. Add eggs and vanilla. Beat well. Mix flour and baking powder together and add to mixture. Add sour cream and mix well. Grease and flour a tube pan. Pour ½ batter into pan and top with ½ of brown sugar and pecan mixture. Pour remaining batter over top and top with remaining brown sugar and pecan mixture. Bake in 350 degree oven for 1 hour. Remove from oven and cool in pan 10 to 15 minutes. Remove and serve.

Funnel Cakes

2	eggs, beaten	1	teaspoon baking powder
1½	cups milk	½	teaspoon salt
2¼	cups flour	2	cups cooking oil

Combine eggs and milk. Sift flour, baking powder and salt together. Add to the egg mixture; beat until smooth with a hand beater. Test to see if the mixture will flow easily through a funnel. If it is too thick, add milk, if it is too thin, add flour. Pour cooking oil into an 8 inch skillet and heat to 360 degrees. Covering the bottom opening of a funnel with your finger, pour a generous ½ cup of batter into the funnel. Hold the end of the funnel close to the surface of the hot oil. Remove finger and release batter into hot oil in a spiral shape. Fry until golden brown, about 3 minutes. Using a spatula, turn the cake carefully and cook for 1 additional minute. Drain on paper towels; sprinkle with powdered sugar or serve hot with syrup. Makes about 20 cakes. BE EXTRA CAREFUL WHEN RELEASING BATTER INTO HOT OIL!

☆

Popcorn Cake

For Popcorn Lovers!

3	quarts popped popcorn	½	pound roasted unsalted
1½	sticks butter		peanuts or regular
¼	cup vegetable oil		peanuts
1	pound miniature	1	pound sugar coated
	marshmallows		chocolate candies

Butter a tube pan. Melt oleo, oil and marshmallows in a large saucepan. Pour popcorn into a large bowl. Add nuts and candies. Pour melted marshmallow mixture over corn, nuts and candies. Mix well, working quickly. Press mixture firmly into pan. Turn cake out immediately onto a large plate. Let "set" overnight for easy cutting. You may also use a 13 x 9 x 2 inch buttered pan and leave in pan for cutting. This cake is great for parties!

Brown Sugar Icebox Cookies

2	sticks oleo, softened	3½	cups flour
2	cups firmly packed dark brown sugar	½	teaspoon salt
		1	teaspoon soda
2	eggs	1	cup chopped pecans
2	teaspoons vanilla		

Cream oleo and sugar together. Add eggs and vanilla. Mix well. Combine flour, salt and soda; add to creamed mixture. Stir in pecans. Roll dough into small 1½ inch diameter jelly rolls. These should be approximately 12 to 18 inches long. Wrap in waxed paper and chill in refrigerator overnight. Remove and slice. Place on lightly greased cookie sheets. Bake at 350 degrees for 12 to 15 minutes. Dough may also be frozen. Remove and let stand at room temperature approximately 15 minutes. Slice and bake.

Bourbon Balls

3	cups crushed vanilla wafers (1 box)	¼	cup cocoa
		½	cup bourbon, brandy, rum or whiskey
¼	cup corn syrup		
2	cups powdered sugar		additional powdered sugar
1	cup chopped pecans		to dip balls in

Mix all ingredients together. Mixture will be dry. Form into small balls and dip in additional powdered sugar. Store in sealed container.

☆

Brownie Drops

2	4-ounce bars German sweet chocolate	¼	teaspoon baking powder
		¼	teaspoon cinnamon
1	tablespoon butter	⅛	teaspoon salt
2	eggs	1	teaspoon vanilla
¾	cup sugar	1	cup chopped pecans
¼	cup flour		

Melt chocolate and butter over low heat. Cool. Beat eggs until foamy. Add sugar, 2 tablespoons at a time, beating until thickened (approximately 5 minutes with electric mixer). Blend in chocolate. Add flour, baking powder, salt and cinnamon; blend. Stir in vanilla and pecans. Drop by teaspoons onto greased baking sheet. Bake at 350 degrees until cookies feel "set" when lightly touched - 8 to 10 minutes. Cool slightly before removing from pan.

Middleton's Famous Brownies

2	cups sugar	1	cup flour
½	cup cocoa	1	teaspoon vanilla
1	cup shortening	1	cup chopped pecans
⅛	teaspoon salt		
4	eggs		
½	cup evaporated milk (can use regular - use 2 tablespoons less)		

Cream first four ingredients together. Add vanilla, eggs, milk and flour. Mix until blended. Add pecans. Grease a 9 x 13 inch pan. Spread mixture evenly into pan and bake at 325 degrees 20 to 30 minutes or until done. Test for doneness by inserting a toothpick through center. Brownies are done when toothpick comes out clean. These are very moist!

Icing:

1	16-ounce box powdered sugar	1	stick oleo
⅛	teaspoon salt, optional	1	tablespoon milk
1	square unsweetened chocolate		

Place oleo in saucepan and melt very slowly over low heat. When melted, stir in chocolate and melt. Pour powdered sugar into a large bowl. Pour chocolate mixture over powdered sugar and stir until blended. Add 1 tablespoon milk. Add a little more if icing is too stiff. Add salt. Spread over brownies while hot. Cool and cut into squares.

Butter Cookies

1	pound butter (no substitution)	¾	cup white granulated sugar
¾	cup brown sugar	4½	cups flour

Cream butter and sugars together. Slowly add flour and mix well. Roll into small balls - 1 inch diameter. Place on ungreased cookie sheet. Bake in 450 degree oven 12 to 15 minutes. Cookies are done when bottom edges are slightly brown. DO NOT OVERBAKE. Remove from pan and cool.

Buffalo Chip Cookies

4	sticks oleo, melted	2	teaspoons cinnamon, optional
2	cups light brown sugar, packed	4	cups flour
2	cups granulated sugar	2	teaspoons baking powder
4	eggs	2	teaspoons baking soda
2	teaspoons vanilla	1	12-ounce bag chocolate chips
2	cups quick cooking oats		
2	cups corn flakes	2	cups chopped pecans

Cream oleo and sugars together. Add eggs and vanilla. Mix together flour, baking powder, baking soda and cinnamon. Add to creamed mixture. Stir in remaining ingredients. Dough will be stiff. Scoop dough with ice cream scoop. Place on lightly greased cookie sheet. Bake in 325 degree oven 15 - 17 minutes. Remove from oven.

☆

Butterfingers

2	cups crispy rice cereal	1	12-ounce package semi - sweet chocolate morsels
2	cups powdered sugar		
1	18-ounce jar crunchy peanut butter	1	teaspoon paraffin
		1	stick margarine

Crunch rice krispies and sugar together. Melt margarine. Add peanut butter and stir. Pour over cereal mixture. Shape into 1 inch balls. Melt chocolate and paraffin on low heat. Dip balls into chocolate and place on waxed paper. Place in refrigerator for 1 hour.

☆

Butterscotch Cookies

1	cup butter or oleo, softened	2½	cups flour
		1	teaspoon baking soda
¾	cup brown sugar	½	teaspoon salt
¾	cup granulated sugar	1	12-ounce package butterscotch morsels
2	eggs		
2	teaspoons vanilla extract		

Cream butter and sugars together. Add eggs and vanilla extract. Mix flour, baking soda and salt together. Add to creamed mixture. Stir in butterscotch morsels. Drop by teaspoons onto ungreased cookie sheet. Bake in 375 degree oven until light brown. Remove and place on wire racks to cool.

Cheesecake Cookies

Crust:
⅔	cup butter	2	cups flour
⅔	cup brown sugar	1	cup chopped pecans

Cream butter and brown sugar. Add flour and pecans and mix with fork until crumbly. Reserve ½ cup for topping. Spread remaining mixture on bottom of cookie sheet. Press evenly and bake in 350 degree oven 12 to 15 minutes or until slightly brown. Remove from oven.

Filling:
2	8-ounce packages cream cheese	4	tablespoons milk
½	cup sugar	2	tablespoons lemon juice
2	eggs	1	teaspoon vanilla

Combine filling ingredients, beat until smooth and spread evenly over cooked mixture. Sprinkle reserved crumb mixture over top. Bake in 350 degree oven for 15 minutes. Cool. Cut into squares. Refrigerate.

☆

Miniature Cheesecakes

2	8-ounce packages cream cheese, softened	1	21-ounce can cherry pie filling
¾	cup sugar	24	foil baking cup liners
2	eggs	24	vanilla wafers
1	teaspoon vanilla		

Place foil baking cup liners in muffin tins. Beat cream cheese, sugar, eggs and vanilla together until smooth. Place a vanilla wafer in each foil cup. Spoon mixture over vanilla wafer. Fill each cup ½ full. Bake at 375 degrees for 12 minutes. Cool in pan. When ready to serve, add a spoonful of pie filling on top of each. These can be made ahead of time and chilled in refrigerator.

Candy Cookies

1	cup shortening	2¼	cups flour
1	cup brown sugar (packed)	1	teaspoon soda
½	cup granulated sugar	½	teaspoon salt
1	teaspoon vanilla	1	16-ounce package sugar
2	teaspoons water		coated chocolate candies
2	eggs		

Cream shortening and sugars. Add vanilla, water and eggs. Mix flour, soda and salt together and add to mixture. Stir in candy. Drop by teaspoonfuls onto ungreased cookie sheet and bake at 375 degrees for 10 to 12 minutes. Cool slightly and remove from pan.

Chocolate Chip Bars

⅔	cup shortening	½	teaspoon soda
2	cups brown sugar	½	teaspoon salt
2	eggs	1	cup chocolate chips
2	teaspoons vanilla	1	cup chopped pecans
2	cups flour		

Cream shortening and sugar. Add eggs and vanilla. Beat well. Sift flour, soda and salt together. Add to creamed mixture. Stir in chocolate chips and pecans. Bake in a greased 9 x 13 inch pan in 350 degree oven 20 to 25 minutes until golden brown. Remove and cool. Cut into squares.

Chocolate Chip Cookies

1	cup butter or margarine, softened	2½	cups flour
		½	teaspoon salt
¾	cup sugar	1	teaspoon baking soda
¾	cup brown sugar	1	12-ounce bag semi - sweet
2	eggs		chocolate chips
2	teaspoons vanilla	1	cup chopped pecans

Cream margarine and sugars. Add eggs and vanilla. Mix flour, salt and baking soda together and add to mixture. Add chocolate chips and pecans. Drop by tablespoons onto ungreased baking sheet. Place 2 inches apart. Bake at 375 degrees 8 to 10 minutes until golden brown. Cool for 2 minutes.

Tiger Cookies

1¾	cups flour	1	teaspoon vanilla
½	teaspoon baking soda	3½	cups sugar frosted flakes
½	teaspoon salt		cereal, crushed to 1½ cups
1	cup oleo, softened	1	6-ounce package semi -
1	cup sugar		sweet chocolate morsels,
2	eggs		melted

Mix sugar and oleo. Beat until light and fluffy. Add eggs and vanilla. Mix baking soda, salt and flour together and add to creamed mixture. Stir in crushed frosted flakes. Drizzle melted chocolate over dough and swirl in gently with a knife. Drop by teaspoonfuls onto ungreased cookie sheet. Bake in 350 degree oven for 12 to 15 minutes. Remove and cool on wire rack. Yields: 5 dozen.

Chocolate Devils

3	cups powdered sugar	¼	cup cocoa
3¾	cups chopped pecans	6	egg whites

Beat egg whites until light and frothy. Mix sugar, pecans and cocoa together. Add to egg whites. Beat lightly. Drop by teaspoonfuls onto lightly greased and floured cookie sheet. Bake in 350 degree preheated oven 20 to 22 minutes. Do not overbake. Cool completely before removing from cookie sheet.

Chocolate Fudge Cookies (Boiled)

2	cups sugar	2½	to 3 cups quick cooking
½	cup milk		oatmeal
1	stick butter or oleo	2	teaspoons vanilla
3	to 4 tablespoons cocoa	1	cup chopped pecans
½	cup peanut butter		

Boil sugar, milk, oleo, and cocoa for 1 to 1½ minutes (start timing after mixture reaches a full rolling boil). Remove from heat, add peanut butter, oatmeal, vanilla and pecans. Beat until blended, then drop by teaspoonfuls onto wax paper. Coconut or dates may be added if desired.

Fudgies

1	package 1 - layer size dark fudge cake mix	½	cup peanut butter flavored pieces
1	8 - ounce carton dairy sour cream	½	cup chopped pecans

Mix cake mix and sour cream together and beat until well blended. Mixture will be smooth. Stir in peanut butter pieces and pecans. Drop by teaspoonfuls onto a greased cookie sheet. Bake in a 350 degree oven 10 - 12 minutes or until set. Remove and cool on wire rack.

Chocolate Peanut Butter Cups

1	15 - ounce roll refrigerated peanut butter cookie dough	48	miniature peanut butter cup candies
		48	pecan halves (optional)

Slice cookie dough into ¾ inch slices. Cut each slice into quarters. Place each quarter, pointed side up, in a greased miniature muffin pan. Bake in 350 degree oven 8 - 10 minutes. Remove from oven and immediately press a peanut butter cup candy gently and evenly into cookie. If desired, when almost cool, place a pecan half on top. Remove from pan. Refrigerate until firm.

Fat Men

1	roll refrigerator chocolate chip cookie dough	32	light caramels
1	6 - ounce package semi - sweet chocolate chips	¼	cup light cream
		1½	cups chopped pecans

Slice cookie dough into ¼ inch thick slices and press in a 9 x 12 x 2 inch pan. Bake for 20 minutes in a 375 degree oven. Remove and cool slightly. Sprinkle chocolate chips over top. Mix light cream and caramels and place over low heat until caramels are melted, stirring constantly. Pour over chocolate chips. Sprinkle pecans over top. Refrigerate. Cut into squares.

Date - Nut Cookies

1	cup sugar	1	cup chopped pecans
1	cup shortening	1	teaspoon vanilla
1	cup brown sugar	1	cup chopped dates
2	eggs, slightly beaten	1	cup corn flakes
2	cups flour	3	tablespoons milk
1	teaspoon soda	⅛	teaspoon salt
2	cups quick cooking oatmeal		

Cream sugar and shortening together. Add brown sugar, eggs, flour, and soda; mix well. Add remaining ingredients. Mix and drop by teaspoonfuls onto greased cookie sheet and bake in 350 degree oven 15 to 20 minutes or until golden brown.

Burton's Frosted Date Balls

1¼	cups sifted flour	1	teaspoon vanilla
¼	teaspoon salt	⅔	cup chopped dates
⅓	cup sifted powdered sugar	1	cup nuts
½	cup oleo, softened		Additional powdered sugar
1	tablespoon milk		to roll balls in

Cream oleo and sugar. Add milk and vanilla. Mix salt and flour together and add to creamed mixture. Add dates and nuts. Roll into small balls and place 3 inches apart on ungreased baking sheet. Bake at 300 degrees until light brown. Remove and roll in additional powdered sugar.

Hello Dollies

1	stick oleo	1	cup chopped pecans
1½	cups crushed graham crackers	1	14 - ounce can sweetened condensed milk
1	cup angel flake coconut		
2	cups semi - sweet chocolate pieces		

Melt oleo in 9 x 9 inch pan. Make layers, by adding remaining ingredients in order listed. Bake in 350 degree oven 20 to 30 minutes or until golden brown. Cool. Cut into squares.

Fruitcake Cookies

2	cups brown sugar	1	teaspoon ground cloves
1	stick oleo	2	ounces whiskey
4	eggs	3	cups chopped pecans
3	tablespoons milk	½	pound candied cherries,
3	teaspoons soda		chopped
3	cups flour	½	pound candied pineapple,
1	teaspoon ground cinnamon		chopped
1	teaspoon ground nutmeg	1	pound raisins

Mix sugar, oleo and eggs. Add milk. Mix spices and soda with 1½ cups flour and add to sugar mixture. Add whiskey and stir. Mix fruit, raisins and nuts in remaining 1½ cups flour and add to first mixture. Dough will be stiff. Drop by teaspoonfuls onto greased cookie sheet and bake in 350 degree oven 15 minutes or until lightly brown. Mop with more whiskey shortly before removing from oven.

Lemon Squares

Crust:

1	cup oleo	2	cups flour
½	cup powdered sugar	½	teaspoon salt

Blend oleo and sugar. Add flour and salt. Mix and press into greased 10 x 13 inch pan. Bake 20 minutes at 325 degrees. While baking, mix the following:

Filling:

4	eggs, lightly beaten	2	cups sugar
	grated rind of 1 lemon	4	tablespoons flour
4	tablespoons lemon juice	1	teaspoon baking powder

Combine filling ingredients; mix and pour over baked crust. Bake an additional 20 to 25 minutes. Remove from oven and cool. Sprinkle with powdered sugar. Cut into squares.

Lemon Coolers

1	box lemon supreme cake mix (dry)	2	cups whipped topping powdered sugar
1	egg		

Mix cake mix, egg and whipped topping together. Drop dough with a teaspoon and roll in powdered sugar. Place on greased cookie sheet and bake in 350 degree oven 8 - 10 minutes. Remove and cool.

Queen's Lemon Nut Icebox Cookies

1	cup shortening	2	cups flour
½	cup granulated sugar	¼	teaspoon salt
½	cup brown sugar	¼	tablespoon soda
1	egg, well beaten	½	cup chopped pecans
2	tablespoons lemon juice		
1	tablespoon grated lemon rind		

Cream shortening and sugars together. Add lemon juice, rind and egg. Mix flour, salt and soda together and add to creamed mixture. Mix well. Stir in pecans. Form dough into shape of a jelly roll approximately 1½ inches in diameter. Wrap in wax paper and chill in refrigerator for at least 2 hours. Place in freezer if desired. Remove when firm. Slice cookies ¼ inch thick and place on lightly greased cookie sheet. Bake at 325 degrees 8 to 10 minutes or until light brown. Remove and cool.

☆

Melting Moments

1	cup butter or margarine, softened	1⅓	cups all - purpose flour red or green sugar crystals or flaked coconut
½	cup powdered sugar		
½	cup cornstarch		

Beat butter and powdered sugar together until light and fluffy. Add flour and cornstarch. Beat until blended. Cover and refrigerate 1 hour. Remove and shape dough into 1 - inch balls. Roll in sugar crystals or coconut. Place 2 - inches apart on ungreased baking sheet. Bake in 325 degree oven for 12 to 15 minutes. Cool 2 to 3 minutes before removing from pan. Yields: 45.

Fast and Fancy Macaroons

1	14 - ounce bag shredded coconut	2	teaspoons vanilla extract
1	14 - ounce can sweetened condensed milk	1	cup chopped almonds (optional)

Combine all ingredients, mixing well. Drop by teaspoonfuls onto well - greased baking sheets. Bake at 350 degrees 10 to 12 minutes or until lightly browned. Remove at once. For special occasions, top with maraschino cherry halves or sprinkle with multi - colored sprinkles or sugar crystals.

Variations:
Chocolate: Fold in 4 squares melted chocolate
Chiparoons: Add 1 cup chocolate chips
Funaroons: Add 8 - 10 drops red or green food coloring

Oatmeal Crisps

2	cups butter	1	teaspoon salt
1	box (2 cups) brown sugar	2	teaspoons soda
2	cups granulated sugar	2	teaspoons cinnamon
2	teaspoons vanilla	5	cups quick oatmeal
4	eggs	1½	cups shredded coconut
3	cups flour	1	cup chopped pecans

Cream butter with sugars. Stir in vanilla. Add eggs and beat. Sift flour, salt, soda and cinnamon. Add to creamed mixture. Stir in oatmeal and coconut; then stir in pecans. Drop by teaspoonfuls onto greased cookie sheet and bake at 350 degrees 10 to 15 minutes. You may also roll dough in jelly roll and wrap in wax paper. Store in freezer until ready to bake. Remove from freezer and let stand at room temperature a few minutes. Slice and place on cookie sheet. Bake 350 degrees 10 to 15 minutes.

Orange Cookies

1½	cups sugar	1	teaspoon soda
1	cup shortening or	1	teaspoon baking powder
	margarine	3¾	cups sifted flour
2	eggs		grated rind of 2 oranges
1	cup sour cream		

Cream sugar and shortening. Add eggs and orange rind. Mix and add sour cream. Mix soda, baking powder and flour together and gradually add to mixture. Drop by teaspoonfuls onto lightly greased cookie sheet. Bake 350 degrees about 15 minutes.

Icing:
2   cups powdered sugar
1   tablespoon melted butter
     juice and rind of 1 orange

Mix together and dip cooled cookies in mixture. Let set.

Orange Fingers

3	cups vanilla wafer crumbs	1	stick butter, melted
1	16 - ounce box powdered	1	cup flaked coconut
	sugar, sifted		
2	cups chopped pecans		
1	6 - ounce can frozen		
	orange juice concentrate,		
	thawed		

Mix vanilla wafer crumbs, powdered sugar and pecans together. Stir in orange juice and butter. Shape into 2 - inch fingers and roll in coconut. Refrigerate. Yields: 4 dozen.

Orange Slice Squares

4	eggs, well beaten	1	package orange slices (18
1	box brown sugar (2½ cups)		- 20), sliced thin
2	cups flour	¼	cup flour to roll orange
1	cup chopped nuts		slices and nuts in
1	teaspoon vanilla		

Roll nuts and orange slices in ¼ cup flour to coat. Set aside. Beat eggs. Add brown sugar and blend well. Add flour and vanilla. Mix well. Add orange slices and nuts. Spread in greased 9 x 9 inch buttered baking dish. Bake in 350 degree oven 15 to 20 minutes or until light golden brown. Remove and cool slightly before cutting into squares.

Surprise Peanut Butter Delights

1	12 - ounce package round buttery crackers	1	package chocolate bark, melted (available in
1	cup smooth or crunchy peanut butter		supermarkets and candy specialty shops)

Spread peanut butter on one cracker and top with another. Repeat until crackers are used. Melt chocolate bark in saucepan. Dip cracker "sandwiches" into chocolate and cover completely. Place on wax paper to dry, about 30 minutes. Makes about 50. Great for parties! No one will ever guess the ingredients!

Peanut Butter Kisses

1	cup butter or oleo	2⅔	cups sifted flour
1	cup sugar	2	teaspoons soda
⅔	cup peanut butter	1	teaspoon salt
1	cup brown sugar	1	14 - ounce package
2	eggs		chocolate kisses
2	teaspoons vanilla		

Cream first four ingredients. Beat eggs and vanilla in a separate bowl and add to mixture. Stir in flour, soda, and salt. Roll into small balls and bake in 350 degree oven 8 to 11 minutes. Remove and place a chocolate kiss in the center. Remove from pan and cool.

Bruce's Peanut Butter Cookies

½	cup shortening	1	tablespoon water
¾	cup brown sugar	1	teaspoon vanilla
½	cup granulated sugar	1	cup flour
1	egg	½	teaspoon soda
1	cup peanut butter (creamy or crunchy)	¼	teaspoon salt

Cream shortening and sugars together. Add egg, peanut butter, water and vanilla. Blend. Mix flour, soda and salt together and add to creamed mixture. Scoop out dough with a teaspoon and roll into a small ball. Place on a greased cookie sheet. Dip fork into water and make a criss - cross design on top of each cookie. You must keep fork wet or will stick to cookie dough. Sprinkle with sugar. Bake in 325 degree oven approximately 15 minutes or until light brown. Remove from oven. Place cookies on wire rack to cool.

☆

Pecan Crispies

½	cup shortening	¼	teaspoon salt
½	cup oleo	½	teaspoon soda
2½	cups brown sugar	1	teaspoon vanilla
2	eggs, slightly beaten	1	cup chopped pecans
2½	cups flour		

Cream shortening, oleo and brown sugar together. Add eggs. Mix flour, salt and soda together. Add to creamed mixture. Add vanilla and pecans. Drop by teaspoonfuls onto greased cookie sheet. Bake in 350 degree oven for 12 minutes. Remove and cool.

Ranger Cookies

2	sticks oleo	2	teaspoons cinnamon
1	cup granulated sugar	1	teaspoon soda
1	cup brown sugar	2	cups uncooked rolled oats
2	eggs	2	cups corn flakes
2	teaspoons vanilla	1	cup coconut
2	cups flour	2	cups chopped pecans
½	teaspoon salt		

Cream oleo and sugars. Add eggs and vanilla. Mix together flour, salt, cinnamon and soda. Add to creamed mixture. Stir in oats, corn flakes, coconut and pecans. Drop by teaspoonfuls onto greased cookie sheet. Bake at 375 degrees for 10 to 12 minutes or until golden brown. Remove and cool on wire rack or paper towels.

Sand Tarts

2	sticks butter, softened	2	teaspoons vanilla
½	cup sifted powdered sugar		additional powdered sugar
2	cups sifted cake flour		to roll baked cookies in
1	cup chopped pecans		

Cream butter and sugar together. Add vanilla, flour and pecans. Dough will be stiff. Shape into small balls and bake on an ungreased cookie sheet in 325 degree oven for 20 minutes. Remove from oven and roll in additional powdered sugar.

Shortbread Cookies

½	cup butter	2	cups flour
½	cup shortening	1	teaspoon baking soda
1	cup sugar	1	cup chopped almonds
2	tablespoons corn syrup	½	teaspoon almond extract
1	teaspoon honey		

Cream butter, shortening and sugar together. Add corn syrup and honey. Mix flour and baking soda together and add to creamed mixture. Stir in almonds and almond extract. Shape into one 1½ x 12 inch log. Wrap in waxed paper and chill in refrigerator 2 hours. Remove and slice into ¼ inch slices. Place on ungreased cookie sheet and bake in 350 degree oven 8 to 10 minutes. Remove and place cookies on wire racks to cool. Yields: 3 dozen.

Snickerdoodles

1	cup shortening	¼	teaspoon cream of tartar
1½	cups sugar	2	tablespoons sugar, set
2	eggs		aside
2¾	cups flour	2	teaspoons cinnamon, set
1	teaspoon baking soda		aside
½	teaspoon salt		

Cream shortening and sugar together. Add eggs and beat well. Add remaining ingredients EXCEPT sugar and cinnamon. Mix well. Chill dough for 2 hours in refrigerator. Roll into small balls and roll in sugar - cinnamon mixture. Place on ungreased cookie sheet. Bake in 400 degree oven for 8 to 10 minutes. Yields: 5 dozen.

Sugar Cookies

1½	cups sugar	1	teaspoon lemon extract
1⅓	cups shortening	4	cups flour
2	eggs	½	teaspoon salt
8	teaspoons milk	3	teaspoons baking powder
1	teaspoon vanilla		

Cream sugar and shortening. Add eggs, milk, vanilla and lemon extract. Mix together flour, salt and baking powder. Add to creamed mixture. Place dough in refrigerator to chill. Divide dough into four sections. Roll out on floured surface and cut with cookie cutter. Place on cookie sheet and sprinkle with sugar. Bake at 375 degrees 8 to 10 minutes. Remove and cool on wire rack or paper towels. Note: Dough can be rolled lengthwise as a jelly roll, wrapped in waxed paper and placed in freezer to chill or freeze. Remove and slice. Place on cookie sheet, sprinkle with sugar and bake 375 degrees 8 to 10 minutes. Remove and cool.

Syrup Teacakes

4½	cups sifted flour	½	cup cooking oil
2	teaspoons soda	¼	cup butter, softened
⅛	teaspoon salt	1½	cups Ribbon Cane syrup
2	teaspoons cinnamon		

Mix oil, butter and syrup together. Mix soda, salt, cinnamon and flour together and add to syrup mixture. Dough will be stiff. Cover and chill in refrigerator 4 to 6 hours. Make several rolls and roll in waxed paper. Chill in refrigerator. Remove and slice. Place on lightly greased cookie sheet. Bake in 350 degree oven for 10 to 15 minutes or until light brown.

Tortilla Cookies

½	cup butter, softened	2	teaspoons cinnamon
1	dozen flour tortillas	1	ounce semi - sweet
1	cup sugar		chocolate, grated

Butter tortillas and place on cookie sheets. Combine sugar and cinnamon; sprinkle over top of tortillas. Bake in preheated 325 degree oven for 15 to 20 minutes or until lightly browned. After removing from oven, sprinkle with chocolate.

Basic Pie Crust

1½	cups flour	⅛	teaspoon salt
½	cup shortening	3	to 6 tablespoons ice water

Mix flour and salt together. Cut in shortening with a fork or pastry blender until mixture is crumbly. Slowly add water, a tablespoon at a time, until dough becomes sticky. Let stand 10 minutes. Roll out on a lightly floured surface. Place pie plate upside down on dough. Cut a circle one inch larger than plate. Carefully lift dough into plate. Flute dough around edges or press edges down tightly. Prick dough with a fork - in bottom of pie shell and around sides. This will keep pastry flat during baking. Bake in 400 degree oven 10 to 12 minutes until light brown. Remove and cool. For fruit and pecan pies, DO NOT PRICK CRUST.

Easy Pie Crust

6	tablespoons oleo, melted	2	tablespoons powdered sugar
1	cup flour		

Melt oleo in pie pan. Mix flour and sugar together and add to oleo. Mix together, using a fork. Press dough in bottom and sides of pan. Bake in a 350 degree oven about 10 minutes or until light brown. Do not overbake.

Water Whipped Pie Crust

¾	cup shortening	1	tablespoon milk
¼	cup plus 2 tablespoons boiling water	2	cups flour
		½	teaspoon salt

Bring water to a boil. Remove from heat. Add milk and shortening. Whip with a fork until smooth and thick. Mix salt and flour together and add to water, milk and shortening mixture. Stir quickly into a dough that clings together. Roll out on a well floured surface. Cut one inch larger than a 9-inch pie pan. Place dough in pan. Bake in 350 degree oven 10 to 15 minutes or until light brown.

Mom's Basic Cream Pie

Crust:
1   8 or 9-inch baked pie crust

Filling:

1	cup sugar	1	teaspoon vanilla
½	cup flour	½	stick oleo
2	cups milk	⅛	teaspoon salt
3	egg yolks		

Separate egg yolks from whites and set whites aside for meringue. Combine sugar, flour and salt. Beat egg yolks and mix with milk. Add to sugar and flour mixture. Stir well. Cook in a double boiler or a non stick saucepan over medium heat. Stir often. Use hand beater to remove any lumps. When very thick, remove from heat and add oleo and vanilla. Cool. Pour into baked pie crust. Top with meringue.

Meringue:

3	egg whites	1	teaspoon vanilla
6	tablespoons powdered sugar		

In a DRY mixing bowl, beat egg whites with an electric mixer until whites form soft peaks. Add vanilla and sugar. Spread over filling. Bake in 350 degree oven until golden brown. Remove. Cool or serve warm.

Variations:
Chocolate: Add 3 tablespoons cocoa to flour and sugar mixture.
Coconut: Add 1 cup coconut to cooked mixture. Sprinkle additional coconut on top of meringue before browning in oven.
Lemon: Add juice and rind of 1 lemon to cooked filling.
Pineapple: Add 1 to 1½ cups drained crushed pineapple to cooked filling.
Banana: Place 1½ to 2 cups sliced bananas in baked pie crust. Pour cooked filling over top. Top with meringue and brown in oven.

☆

Dutch Apple Pie

1   8 or 9-inch unbaked pie
     crust

Filling:

5   large apples, peeled and   2   teaspoons cinnamon
     sliced   2   tablespoons flour
½   cup sugar

Mix sugar, cinnamon and flour together. Add to sliced apples to cover well. Pour into unbaked pie crust. Cover with topping. Press down and seal edges. Bake at 425 degrees in preheated oven for 10 minutes. Turn temperature down to 350 degrees and continue baking for 30 more minutes. Remove from oven.

Topping:

½   cup sugar   1   stick oleo, melted
1   cup flour

Melt oleo and mix with sugar and flour.

☆

Cowboy Cherry Pie

1   graham cracker crust   1   9-ounce carton whipped
1   21-ounce can cherry pie   topping
     filling, chilled

Pour chilled pie filling into pie crust. Top with whipped topping. May also use blueberry or strawberry pie filling. Refrigerate.

Cheesecake Pie

Crust:

1¼ cups graham cracker crumbs	¼ cup oleo, melted

Combine crumbs and oleo. Mix well and press into buttered 8-inch pie plate.

Filling:

1 8-ounce package cream cheese (softened)	1 teaspoon vanilla
½ cup sugar	2 eggs
1 tablespoon lemon juice	dash of salt

Beat cream cheese until fluffy. Gradually add sugar, lemon juice, vanilla and salt. Add eggs, one at a time, beating well after each addition. Pour filling into crumb crust. Bake in 325 degree oven 25 to 30 minutes or until "set". Remove from oven. Spread topping over top and bake an additional 10 minutes. Cool. Refrigerate 4 to 6 hours or overnight.

Topping:

1 cup sour cream	1 teaspoon vanilla
2 tablespoons sugar	

Mix together.

☆

Chocolate Chip Pie

1 cup chocolate chips (semi-sweet)	1 cup sugar
½ cup margarine, melted	1½ cups chopped pecans
½ cup flour	2 teaspoons vanilla
2 eggs slightly beaten	1 unbaked 9-inch pie shell

Mix flour and sugar together and set aside. In another bowl, slightly beat eggs with a fork. Add melted margarine and vanilla. Stir with a fork. Add flour and sugar mixture, chocolate chips and pecans. Mix well and pour into unbaked pie shell. Bake 45 minutes at 350 degrees. Serve with a scoop of ice cream on top.

Fudge Pie

1	stick oleo	2	beaten eggs
1½	squares unsweetened chocolate	½	cup flour
		1	teaspoon vanilla
1	cup sugar	½	cup chopped pecans
⅛	teaspoon salt		

Melt oleo and chocolate over low heat on top of stove in 9-inch pie pan. Remove from heat and add sugar and salt. Stir until blended. Add remaining ingredients and stir well. Bake in 325 degree oven for 30 minutes. Remove and serve warm with a scoop of vanilla ice cream on top.

☆

Grasshopper Pie

Crust:

2	tablespoons melted butter	18	crushed chocolate sandwich cookies

Combine and press in pie plate.

Filling:

24	large marshmallows	2	tablespoons white crème de cocoa
½	cup milk		
4	tablespoons green crème de menthe	1	cup whipping cream, whipped

Melt marshmallows in milk over low heat. Remove from heat and add crème de menthe and crème de cocoa. Chill in refrigerator. Fold in whipped cream and pour into pie shell. Freeze. Serve frozen.

Chocolate Bar Pie

1	graham cracker crust or regular baked pie crust	8	ounces milk chocolate with almonds candy bar
1	16-ounce container whipped topping, thawed		

Break candy into small pieces and melt slowly over low heat. Remove and add to ⅔ of the whipped topping. Mix well. Pour into baked pie crust. Spread remaining whipped topping over top. Refrigerate overnight.

☆

Lime Chiffon Pie

4	beaten egg yolks (save whites and set aside)	2	teaspoons grated lemon rind
¾	cup sugar	½	cup sugar
¼	cup lime juice	4	stiffly beaten egg whites
¼	cup lemon juice	1	9-inch baked pie shell
⅛	teaspoon salt	1	8-ounce carton whipped topping
1	tablespoon unflavored gelatin		drops of green food coloring
¼	cup cold water		

Separate egg yolks from whites and set whites aside. Combine egg yolks, ¾ cup sugar, lime juice, lemon juice and salt. Cook in double boiler or over very low heat in non stick saucepan until thick, beating constantly with hand beater. Stir gelatin in cold water until dissolved. Add to mixture and stir until dissolved. Add lemon rind and cool mixture until almost set. Beat egg whites and fold in remaining half cup sugar. Fold into cooled mixture. Add a few drops of green food coloring. Pour into baked pie shell. Chill in refrigerator until firm. Spread with whipped topping. Store in refrigerator.

Lemon Icebox Pie

1	8-inch graham cracker crust	2	egg yolks
1	14-ounce can sweetened condensed milk	¼	cup fresh lemon juice
		1	8-ounce carton whipped topping

Mix milk, yolks and lemon juice together. Pour into pie crust. Top with whipped topping. Refrigerate overnight.

Peach Icebox Pie

1	9-inch baked pie crust	1	cup chopped pecans
1	8-ounce package cream cheese, softened	1	cup whipping cream, whipped
½	cup powdered sugar		
4	cups sliced peaches, fresh (if using canned, drain well)		

Blend cream cheese and powdered sugar together. Spread evenly over pie crust. Pour peaches over cream cheese mixture. Sprinkle pecans over peaches and top with whipping cream. Refrigerate 4 to 6 hours or overnight.

Angel Pecan Pie

3	egg whites	1	teaspoon vanilla
2	teaspoons baking powder	1	cup chopped pecans
1	cup sugar	1	8-ounce carton whipped topping
14	double graham crackers, crushed		

Beat egg whites until frothy. Add baking powder and sugar. Beat until stiff, but not dry. Fold in crushed graham crackers, pecans and vanilla. Pour into a buttered pie pan and bake in 350 degree oven for 30 minutes. Remove and cool. Top with whipped topping and chill 4 to 6 hours or overnight.

Pecan Tassies (Miniature Pecan Pies)

Dough:

1	6-ounce package cream cheese, softened	1	cup oleo (2 sticks)
		2	cups sifted flour

Cream cheese and oleo together. Blend in flour. Chill dough in refrigerator for 1 hour.

Filling:

2	tablespoons oleo	2	eggs
1½	cups brown sugar	2	tablespoons light corn
3	teaspoons vanilla		syrup
⅛	teaspoon salt	1½	cups chopped pecans

Cream oleo and brown sugar. Add eggs. Mix together and add vanilla, salt, syrup and pecans. To form crusts, make 48 small balls from chilled dough. Place in miniature muffin tins and spread on bottom and around sides. Place approximately 1½ teaspoons filling in each tin. Bake at 350 degrees for 12 to 15 minutes. Remove immediately from muffin tin. Cool.

☆

Southern Pecan Pie

1	cup white corn syrup	1	cup pecans, halves or
1	cup brown sugar		chopped
⅓	cup melted butter		pinch of salt
3	whole eggs, beaten	1	unbaked 8 or 9-inch pie
1	teaspoon vanilla		shell

Beat eggs well and add remaining ingredients. Pour into unbaked pie shell and bake in preheated 350 degree oven approximately 50 to 60 minutes or until set. Top will slightly crack. Remove from oven and cool.

Millionaire Pie

1	9-inch graham cracker pie crust	1	cup chopped pecans
1	14-ounce can condensed milk	¼	cup lemon juice
1	20-ounce can crushed pineapple, drained	1	9-ounce container whipped cream

Mix all ingredients together and pour into pie crust. Chill 3 to 4 hours or overnight. Serves 6 to 8.

Pumpkin Praline Pie

Praline Layer:

⅓	cup brown sugar	⅓	cup finely chopped pecans
2	tablespoons soft butter		

Blend together brown sugar, butter and pecans. Press into a 9-inch un-baked pie shell.

Filling:

2	eggs	½	teaspoon cinnamon
1	16-ounce can pumpkin	½	teaspoon ginger
⅔	cup brown sugar	½	teaspoon salt
1	tablespoon flour	1	cup light cream
¼	teaspoon cloves		whipping cream for
⅛	teaspoon mace		topping

Beat eggs until frothy, then add remaining ingredients in order given. Pour over praline layer and bake in preheated oven 400 degrees for 50 to 55 minutes or until tip of sharp knife comes out clean. Cool and serve with whipping cream on top.

M. P.'s Strawberry Pie

1	8-inch graham cracker crust	1	12-ounce carton whipped topping
1	8-ounce package cream cheese, softened		
½	cup powdered sugar		
1	pint fresh strawberries, sliced or 1 pint frozen strawberries, WELL DRAINED		

Cream cheese. Add sugar and strawberries. Fold in whipped topping. Pour into crust and chill in refrigerator.

Sweet Potato Pie

2	cups cooked, mashed sweet potatoes	⅛	teaspoon salt
2	cups sugar	1	teaspoon cinnamon
4	eggs	½	teaspoon nutmeg
1	5-ounce can evaporated milk	½	teaspoon ginger
1	stick oleo, melted	1	teaspoon vanilla
		1	unbaked pie crust

Mix well in order listed. Beat well and pour into unbaked pie crust. Bake in 350 degree oven for 1 hour.

☆

Apple Crisp

4	large apples, peeled and sliced	1	teaspoon cinnamon
1	cup brown sugar	1	stick oleo, softened or melted
1	cup flour		

Place apples in a 9-inch baking dish. Mix flour, sugar and cinnamon together. Add oleo, mixing with a fork until crumbly. Sprinkle on top of apples and bake in a 400 degree oven 30 to 35 minutes until brown.

Blueberry Cobbler

| 2 | 21-ounce cans blueberry pie filling | 1 | egg |
| 1 | 18½-ounce box white cake mix | ½ | cup softened margarine |

Spread pie filling in 13 x 9 x 2 inch baking pan. Cream margarine. Add cake mix and egg. Blend well. Mixture will be stiff. Spoon over filling. Bake in preheated 350 degree oven 40 to 45 minutes or until golden brown.

Cherry Crisp

| 2 | 21-ounce cans cherry pie filling | 1½ | sticks margarine |
| 3 | cups yellow cake mix (1 box) | 2 | cups pecans (chopped) |

Grease a 9 x 13 inch baking dish. Pour pie filling in bottom of dish. Sprinkle cake mix over top. Dot with margarine and cover with pecans. Bake in 350 degree oven for 40 minutes.

East Texas Dewberry Cobbler

3	to 4 cups fresh dewberries	4	teaspoons cornstarch
1½	cups sugar		pastry for 2 pie crusts
1½	sticks butter		butter and sugar for
1	teaspoon vanilla		topping

Rinse berries well. Add sugar to berries and place in saucepan. Cover with water and bring to a boil. Simmer for 3 minutes. Add butter and vanilla and cook 2 more minutes. Place 5 to 6 tablespoons berry juice in a bowl and add cornstarch. Blend until smooth. Add to berry mixture. Simmer until slightly thickened. Place 1 recipe pie crust in a 2 x 6 x 10 inch baking dish. Pour berry mixture over crust. Cover with 1 recipe pie crust that is cut into strips. Dot with butter and sprinkle sugar over top. Bake in 350 degree oven 50 to 60 minutes. Serves: 8.

Peach Cobbler

Filling:

1	29-ounce can sliced peaches	½	cup sugar
		1	cup water

Mix peaches, water and sugar together in a saucepan. Place over heat and bring to a boil. Boil 5 minutes. Pour into a 9 x 13 inch dish.

Pastry:

1	cup flour	½	stick margarine, melted (to brush on top of pastry)
1	tablespoon sugar		
	dash of salt	¼	cup sugar to sprinkle on top of pastry
⅓	cup shortening		
2	tablespoons ice water (more if needed)		

Combine flour, 1 tablespoon sugar and salt together. Cut in shortening until consistency of cornmeal. Slowly add ice water and stir until dough holds its shape. Roll out on a floured surface. Cut into strips. Crisscross strips over filling. Brush pastry with melted margarine. Sprinkle with ¼ cup sugar. Bake in a 400 degree oven 30 minutes or until golden brown. Serves 6 to 8.

☆

Rich Banana Pudding

6	bananas, sliced	3	cups cold milk
1	14-ounce can sweetened condensed milk	2	(4-serving size) packages instant vanilla pudding
1	12-ounce box vanilla wafers	1	12-ounce carton frozen whipped topping, thawed

Line the bottom and sides of a 13 x 9 x 2 inch dish with vanilla wafers. Cover completely with sliced bananas. Prepare pudding according to package directions using the 3 cups cold milk. Add sweetened condensed milk. Fold in whipped topping. Pour over bananas. Chill in refrigerator. Serves 10 to 12.

Four Layer Delight

First Layer:

1	cup flour	1	cup chopped pecans
1	stick butter, melted		

Mix well and press into a 9 x 9 x 2 inch pan. Bake in 350 degree oven for 20 minutes. Remove and cool.

Second Layer:

1	8-ounce package cream cheese, softened	1	cup powdered sugar
		1	cup whipped topping

Mix together and spread over first cooled layer.

Third Layer:

1	3-ounce package vanilla instant pudding mix	2½	cups cold milk
1	3-ounce package choco- late instant pudding mix		

Mix together and beat for 2 minutes. Spread over second layer.

Fourth Layer:

1	9½-ounce carton whipped topping	1	cup chopped pecans

Spread whipped topping over third layer and sprinkle chopped pecans over top. Refrigerate overnight.

☆

Apricot Balls

1   8-ounce package dried
    apricots, chopped fine
1   14-ounce can sweetened
    condensed milk
1   cup shredded coconut

1½ cups chopped pecans
1   teaspoon lemon juice
    powdered sugar to roll
    balls in

Mix first five ingredients together and form into small balls. Roll in powdered sugar. Refrigerate.

Christmas Hard Candy

3   cups sugar
1   cup light corn syrup
1   cup water

1   teaspoon oil base flavoring
    food coloring
    powdered sugar

Cook sugar, water and syrup until it reaches 310 degrees. Remove from heat. Add flavoring and food coloring. Pour on foil that has been covered with powdered sugar. Let harden and break into pieces. Store in airtight container.

Date Nut Candy

3   cups sugar
1   cup evaporated milk
1   pound package pitted
    dates, chopped

1½ cups chopped pecans
1   teaspoon vanilla
    powdered sugar

Mix sugar and milk in a saucepan. Boil until forms a soft ball. Add dates and vanilla. Cook approximately 3 more minutes. Remove and beat until thick. Add pecans. Thoroughly wet a cloth and lay on counter. Pour candy into a log shape on the wet cloth. Roll up in the cloth. Let sit for 1 hour. Unroll, slice and dip in powdered sugar if desired.

Divinity

½	cup light corn syrup	2	egg whites
2½	cups sugar	1	teaspoon vanilla
¼	teaspoon salt	1	cup coarsely chopped nuts
½	cup water		(walnuts or pecans)

Combine syrup, sugar, salt and water in saucepan. Cook over medium heat, stirring constantly until sugar dissolves. Cook without stirring to a firm ball stage- 248 degrees. While cooking, in a separate bowl, beat egg whites until stiff but not dry. When candy reaches 248 degrees, slowly pour half of mixture over egg whites, beating constantly. Cook remaining mixture until it spins a thread. Add this slowly to first mixture, beating constantly. Continue beating until mixture holds its shape. Add vanilla and nuts. Drop by teaspoonfuls onto waxed paper. (Spinning a thread is done by dipping a spoon into mixture and slowly pouring it back into saucepan.) Be patient!

☆

Chocolate Truffles

1	cup whipping cream (not whipped)	½	stick butter
		1	teaspoon vanilla
12	ounces semi-sweet chocolate, chopped		powdered sugar

Heat cream in a small saucepan. Do not boil. Remove from heat and stir in chocolate, butter and vanilla. Stir until smooth. Pour mixture onto a dry cookie sheet and chill in refrigerator 3-4 hours. Remove and using a teaspoon, scoop candy into 1 inch mounds. Coat in powdered sugar and roll into balls. Place on cookie sheet and chill in refrigerator until firm. Coat with desired coatings. Yields: 48.

Coatings:
Melted Chocolate
Melted White Chocolate
Melted White Chocolate,
tinted with food coloring
Coconut (plain or toasted)
Chopped nuts
Powdered Sugar

Double-Decker Fudge

1 cup chocolate chips	2½ cups sugar
1 cup peanut butter chips	1 7-ounce jar marshmallow
¾ cup evaporated milk	creme
3 tablespoons butter	2 teaspoons vanilla

Place peanut butter chips and chocolate chips in separate bowls.Combine milk, butter, sugar and marshmallow creme in a heavy 3-quart saucepan. Cook over medium heat, stirring constantly. When mixture begins to boil, continue cooking and stirring for 5 minutes. Remove from heat. Add vanilla. Add half of mixture to peanut butter chips, stirring until chips are melted. Pour this mixture into a greased 9-inch square pan. Add remaining marshmallow mixture to chocolate chips. Stir until chips are melted. Spread over top of peanut butter layer. Cool in refrigerator. Cut into squares. Store in refrigerator.

☆

Good Fudge

4½ cups sugar	1 14-ounce can condensed
2 sticks oleo	milk
1 16-ounce bag chocolate	1 7-ounce jar marshmallow
chips	creme
2 cups chopped pecans or	
walnuts	

Combine sugar, oleo and milk in a saucepan. Cook over medium heat. Bring to a boil and boil for 3 minutes. Remove from heat and stir in chocolate chips, nuts and marshmallow creme. Stir well. Pour into a 13 x 9 x 2-inch buttered pan. Cool and cut into squares.

☆

Maple Walnut Fudge

3 cups packed light brown	1 cup chopped walnuts
sugar	1 teaspoon vanilla extract
1 can evaporated milk-⅔ cup	1 teaspoon maple extract
4 tablespoons butter	

Mix sugar, milk and butter in a heavy saucepan. Bring to a boil, stirring constantly, over medium heat. Boil, without stirring, 3 minutes or 234 to 240 degrees on a candy thermometer (soft ball stage). Remove and let sit until cools down to 110 degrees. Add remaining ingredients. Stir well and spread into a 9-inch buttered square pan. Refrigerate until firm (about 6 to 8 hours). Cut into squares.

Microwave Fudge

1	pound powdered sugar	¼	cup milk
½	cup unsweetened cocoa powder	1	cup chopped nuts
1	stick butter	2	teaspoons vanilla

Mix sugar and cocoa together and pour into a 10-inch square glass dish. Cut butter into small pieces and place over sugar mixture. Pour milk over mixture. DO NOT STIR. Microwave on high until bubbly, about 2 or 3 minutes. Remove and stir to mix well. Add nuts and vanilla. Stir and distribute evenly in dish. Refrigerate for 1 hour or until firm. Cut into pieces.

☆

Tiger Butter

1	pound white chocolate	1	pound semi-sweet chocolate, melted
1	12-ounce jar chunky peanut butter		

Mix white chocolate and peanut butter together in top of a double boiler; bringing water to a boil. Turn heat to low and cook until melted, stirring constantly. Pour onto buttered 10 x 15 x 1-inch jelly roll pan. Pour semi-sweet chocolate over mixture and swirl through with a knife. Chill in refrigerator until firm. Cut into squares. Store in refrigerator.

☆

Red Peanut Patties

2	cups sugar	¼	teaspoon red food coloring
½	cup corn syrup	1	stick margarine
½	cup evaporated milk		
2½	to 3 cups raw shelled peanuts		

Mix sugar, corn syrup, milk and peanuts together. Cook over medium heat until firm ball stage. Remove and add margarine and food coloring. Beat until loses gloss. Drop candy into 4 inch patties onto waxed paper. Cool.

Peanut Clusters

| 1 | 8-ounce package semi-sweet chocolate pieces | 8 | ounces Spanish peanuts |

Place chocolate pieces in top of a double boiler, over hot water. Do not boil. Melt chocolate. Remove from heat and add peanuts. Stir and drop by teaspoonfuls onto waxed paper. Chill in refrigerator 4 to 6 hours. Store in cool place. Yields: 2½ dozen clusters.

Peanut Butter Fudge

1	cup evaporated milk	1	12-ounce jar peanut butter (chunky or smooth)
½	stick butter		
2	cups sugar	2	teaspoons vanilla
1	cup miniature marshmallows		

Combine milk, butter and sugar in a saucepan and bring to a boil. Boil for 5 minutes, stirring constantly. Remove from heat and stir in peanut butter, marshmallows and vanilla. Stir until blended. Pour into a 9-inch square buttered pan. Cool. Cut into squares.

Famous Peanut Brittle

3	cups sugar	3	teaspoons butter
½	cup water	2	teaspoons soda
1	cup white corn syrup	1	teaspoon salt
3	cups raw peanuts	1	teaspoon vanilla

Boil sugar, water and syrup until spins thread. This is done by taking a teaspoon of syrup mixture and holding above pan, slowly pouring back into mixture. A thin thread will spin off spoon. This first step takes about 10 minutes. Add peanuts and stir constantly. Cook until mixture turns a golden brown. Remove from heat. Add butter, salt, vanilla and soda. Mixture will foam. Stir to mix quickly and pour onto a large buttered cookie sheet. When candy is cool, break into pieces.

Kisses

1	cup brown sugar	1	cup chopped pecans
1	egg white		

Beat egg white until stiff. Add sugar and pecans. Drop by teaspoonfuls onto ungreased cookie sheet. Bake at 250 degrees for 30 minutes. Remove from oven and remove from cookie sheet immediately or will stick. Run spatula under running water before lifting each kiss off sheet. Cool.

Millionaire Candy

1	pound caramels	8	ounces chocolate candy
2	cups pecan halves	⅕	section paraffin wax
3½	tablespoons milk		

Place caramels and milk in a saucepan and place over low heat. When caramels are melted, remove from heat. Add pecans and stir. Drop by teaspoonfuls onto a buttered cookie sheet. Cool. Melt chocolate candy and paraffin wax together. Dip caramel pieces into chocolate. Cool on buttered tray.

Pecan Roll

1	cup brown sugar	1	cup evaporated milk
2	cups sugar	2	cups chopped pecans
½	cup light corn syrup		

Combine sugars, corn syrup and milk in a saucepan. Place over medium heat and cook only until sugars dissolve to soft ball stage, 236 degrees. Remove and cool to lukewarm, without stirring. Beat until candy holds its shape. Cool completely and shape in two 1½ inch rolls. Roll in pecans. Press pecans into candy. Chill in refrigerator. Slice. Yields: 30 slices.

Creamy Pralines

2	cups sugar	1	cup buttermilk
1	teaspoon soda		

Mix sugar, soda and buttermilk in a large saucepan. Cook over medium heat, stirring occasionally, until light brown.

Add:

2	tablespoons margarine	1	teaspoon vanilla
2½	cups chopped pecans		pinch salt

Stir well and continue cooking, stirring constantly until soft ball stage. Remove from heat. Stir 2 or 3 minutes until slightly firm and still glossy. Quickly drop by teaspoons onto buttered waxed paper or foil. Will harden quickly. Note: If candy does not hold its shape, beat a few more minutes until firmer.

Hurst's Pecan Candy Squares

2	cups sugar	1	cup light brown sugar
1⅓	cups light corn syrup	1	cup light cream
1	14-ounce can evaporated milk	½	pound butter
		6	cups chopped pecans

Combine all ingredients except pecans in a heavy saucepan. Cook, stirring often until small amount of mixture forms a hard ball when dropped in cold water (246 degrees on candy thermometer). Remove from heat and let cool slightly. Mix well with a spoon for 2 or 3 minutes. (Mixture will not be smooth.) Stir in pecans. Pour into buttered 13 x 9 x 2-inch pan. Smooth top with hand. Cool completely and cut in 1½-inch squares. Wrap each piece in foil or plastic wrap. Makes about 60 pieces.

Penuche

2	cups brown sugar	1	cup chopped pecans
¾	cup milk	2	tablespoons butter
1	teaspoon vanilla		

Place sugar and milk in a saucepan and cook over low heat, stirring constantly. Remove from heat when mixture reaches soft ball stage. Stir in vanilla, pecans and butter. Beat until creamy and pour into a 9 x 9 inch buttered pan. Cool. Cut into squares.

Haystacks

1   6-ounce package semi-   1   3-ounce can chow mein
    sweet chocolate pieces   noodles

Slowly melt chocolate pieces in a medium bowl in microwave at medium or low for 3 to 4 minutes. Stir until smooth. Add noodles and using 2 forks, toss to coat well. Form into 1 to 2 inch clusters on foil or wax paper. Cool to set.

Pretzel Candy

1   pound white chocolate   1   cup broken pretzel sticks
1   cup salted or unsalted
    peanuts (not Spanish
    peanuts)

Melt chocolate in double boiler. Quickly stir nuts and pretzels into melted chocolate. Stir well. Quickly drop by teaspoonfuls onto ungreased cookie sheet. Let harden.

Spiders

1   6-ounce package   1   8-ounce can peanuts
    chocolate chips   1   small can chow mein
1   8-ounce package   noodles
    butterscotch chips

Melt chips in top of double boiler. Pour over nuts and noodles to cover. Drop by spoonfuls onto wax paper.

Strawberry Candies

2	3-ounce packages straw-berry gelatin	1	teaspoon vanilla
1½	cups pecans, chopped fine		red and green decorators sugar
1	cup shredded coconut		slivered almonds
¾	cup condensed milk		

Mix gelatin, pecans and coconut together. Add condensed milk and vanilla. Stir well. Chill in refrigerator 1 hour. Shape into strawberries. Roll in red decorator sugar. Dot the end of each in green, decorator sugar. Place a piece of slivered almond in end of each for stem.

English Toffee

1	stick oleo	1½	tablespoons water
1	stick butter	½	cup slivered almonds
1	cup plus 1 tablespoon sugar	1	12-ounce package semi-sweet chocolate chips

Mix oleo, butter, sugar and water together in a saucepan. Boil over medium heat to 250 degrees. Add almonds and stir constantly until candy reaches 300 degrees. Remove from heat and pour onto a buttered cookie sheet. When partially cool, melt ½ package chocolate chips and spread over candy. Place in refrigerator to cool. Remove and turn candy over. Melt remaining chocolate chips and spread over candy. Return to refrigerator to cool. Break into pieces and store in airtight container.

Freezer Ice Cream

6	eggs	2	12 - ounce cans evapo-
1½	cups sugar		rated milk
4	teaspoons vanilla	½	gallon milk
1	14 - ounce can condensed milk		

Beat eggs until frothy. Add sugar and beat. Add evaporated milk, condensed milk and vanilla. Pour into gallon - size freezer and add ½ gallon milk. Stir well. Cover container tightly. Pack freezer with crushed ice and ice cream salt. Turn freezer until hard. Serve.

Fresh Peach Ice Cream

6	eggs	2	cups sugar
1	14 - ounce can sweetened condensed milk	4	teaspoons vanilla
		3	cups thinly sliced peaches (fresh)
1	12 - ounce can evaporated milk		milk to fill freezer container

Beat eggs until light and fluffy. Add evaporated milk, condensed milk, sugar, vanilla and peaches. Stir well and pour into a 4-quart or 5-quart container. Fill with milk to fill line. Stir well. Freeze according to freezer directions, using ice and ice cream salt to freeze.

Orange Sherbet

2	quarts orange soda	1	20 - ounce can crushed
2	14 - ounce cans sweetened condensed milk		pineapple

Mix together and pour into gallon - size ice cream freezer. Cover container. Pack freezer with crushed ice and ice cream salt. Turn freezer until hard to turn. Serve.

☆ INDEX ☆

INDEX

INDEX

MEXICAN DISHES

N

O

P

INDEX

Star-Daze Productions
1526 Mabry Mill
Houston, Texas 77062

Please send ____ copies of MAN IN THE KITCHEN TEXAS STYLE! at
$9.95 plus $1.50 postage and handling per copy. Texas residents add $.82
each for tax.
Make checks payable to Star-Daze Productions.

Please mail to:

Name _____
Address _____
City _____State _____Zip _____

— —

Star-Daze Productions
1526 Mabry Mill
Houston, Texas 77062

Please send ____ copies of MAN IN THE KITCHEN TEXAS STYLE! at
$9.95 plus $1.50 postage and handling per copy. Texas residents add $.82
each for tax.
Make checks payable to Star-Daze Productions.

Please mail to:

Name _____
Address _____
City _____State _____Zip

— —

Star-Daze Productions
1526 Mabry Mill
Houston, Texas 77062

Please send ____ copies of MAN IN THE KITCHEN TEXAS STYLE! at
$9.95 plus $1.50 postage and handling per copy. Texas residents add $.82
each for tax.
Make checks payable to Star-Daze Productions.

Please mail to:

Name _____
Address _____
City _____State _____Zip _____